LOGICAL ABILITIES IN CHILDREN

VOLUME I
ORGANIZATION OF LENGTH AND CLASS CONCEPTS:
EMPIRICAL CONSEQUENCES OF A
PIAGETIAN FORMALISM

CHILD PSYCHOLOGY

A series of volumes edited by **David S. Palermo**

LOGICAL ABILITIES IN CHILDREN

BY DANIEL N. OSHERSON

STANFORD UNIVERSITY

VOLUME I

ORGANIZATION OF LENGTH AND CLASS CONCEPTS:
EMPIRICAL CONSEQUENCES OF A PIAGETIAN FORMALISM

 LAWRENCE ERLBAUM ASSOCIATES, PUBLISHERS

1974   Potomac, Maryland

DISTRIBUTED BY THE HALSTED PRESS DIVISION OF

JOHN WILEY & SONS
New York   Toronto   London   Sydney

Lawrence Erlbaum Associates, Publishers
12736 Lincolnshire Drive,
Potomac, Maryland 20854

Distributed solely by Halsted Press Division,
John Wiley & Sons, Inc., New York

Library of Congress Cataloging in Publication Data

Osherson, Daniel N.
    Logical abilities in children.

    (Child Psychology)
    Includes bibliographic references.
    CONTENTS: v.1. Organization of length
and class concepts: empirical consequences
of a Piagetian formalism.
    1. Child study. 2. Learning ability. 3.
Cognition (Child psychology) I. Title. II Series.

LB1134.084   155.4'13   74-2298
ISBN 0-470-65723-5

Printed in the United States of America

CONTENTS

PREFACE

Many psychologists agree with the following statements: (*a*) The writings of Jean Piaget constitute a tremendously useful and interesting account of intellectual development. (*b*) A psychological theory—like any scientific theory—should allow the derivation of predictions that are sufficiently unambiguous to make clear what evidence would disconfirm the theory. And (*c*) Piaget's theory is far too vague to generate the nontrivial and precise predictions necessary to test it. This book is an attempt to resolve the "dissonance" associated with these three propositions.

Piaget's "grouping" model for concrete operational thought is the starting point. After a brief examination of Piaget's formulation of it, an axiomatization of the grouping due to the logician Jean-Blaise Grize is presented. Grize's axiom-system is then converted, by stages, into a theory of children's understanding of length and class-inclusion concepts. The predictions of this theory are tested in two experiments. Grize's axiomatization of the grouping stems from what Piaget calls "genetic epistemology." However, the theory presented here, although built on Grize's work, is purely psychological in intent.

The material in this book provided the basis for a master's thesis submitted to the Department of Psychology of the University of Pennsylvania. Its publication was delayed for two years while I explored other approaches to the development of logical thinking in children. One of these alternative approaches is presented in Volume II. To my mind, the theory of Volume II shows that the theory of Volume I is irretrievably mistaken in outlook. Still, some examples of incorrect approaches are valuable, as I hope this one is.

It is a pleasure to acknowledge and thank Rochel Gelman, Burton Rosner, and David Williams for encouragement and excellent advice throughout the project reported in Volume I. Conversations with the following people were also profitable: Justin Aronfreed, Brian Chellas, Deborah Kemler, Michael Levine, Ellen Markman, Samuel Osherson, and Harris Savin. The misjudgments that remain in the work are my responsibility. Pamela Freeman helped collect the data. The manuscript was expertly and graciously typed by Isabelle Friedman. The research reported in this volume was supported by NIHCD Grant No. 04598 to Rochel Gelman.

1
INTRODUCTION

1. BACKGROUND OF THE PROBLEM

Preadolescent children's understanding of the logic of class and length relationships has received considerable attention since Piaget's pioneering investigations (Inhelder & Piaget, 1964; Piaget, 1965; Piaget & Inhelder, 1967; Piaget, Inhelder & Szeminska, 1960). Piaget reports that children less than 7–8 years of age (approximately) are unable to solve problems requiring fundamental class-inclusion and length concepts. Older children solve them with little difficulty. He characterizes the younger children as *preoperational,* and the older as *operational.*

A review of the research in this area is impossible here. Instead, we describe four representative paradigms utilized by Piaget and others to investigate children's understanding of class-inclusion and length principles. In this way the "uninitiated" reader will get some idea of the previous work done on the topic. Later we discuss some of Piaget's theoretical ideas which relate to the experiments.

Classification of objects

Inhelder and Piaget (1964) presented children 2 to 10 years old a collection of blocks of various shapes, sizes, and colors. The children were told to "put together the things which are alike,"

1

or "the same as each other," etc. The authors report that before a true classification can be achieved—one that conforms to ten principles of true classification, such as exhaustion and hierarchization of the elements (Inhelder & Piaget, 1964, p. 48) — children first pass through two immature stages.

The first stage is called "graphic collections," during which the spatial arrangement of the elements to be classified bears heavily on the subject's opinion as to what elements go together. For example, the four-year-old child may place a triangle over a square because the ensemble reminds him of a house.

Intermediate between graphic collections and true classification is a stage called "nongraphic collections." Children in this second stage still fail to grasp the hierarchical nature of true classification. Suppose that a class B can be partitioned into two subclasses, A and A'. According to the authors, "a child understands inclusion if he is capable of grasping that 'all' the A are 'some' of the B, while we do not have inclusion if the child understands the statement 'All the A are B . . . ' (for instance, all the circles are blue) as being equivalent to 'All the A are all the B.' (Thus a stage II child will deny that all the circles are blue 'because there are also blue squares.') [p. 50]."

Kofsky (1966) attempted to replicate the stage-sequence findings reported by Inhelder and Piaget (1964), but met with only moderate success. Vygotsky (1962) and Bruner, Olver, and Greenfield (1966) studied the problem of children's classification from an alternative and interesting approach.

Additive Composition of Classes

Piaget (1965) reports an experiment designed to investigate children's understanding of the principle that the number of elements in a (nonempty) finite class is always greater than that of any subclass properly included in it. The experiment is described as follows: "We took, for instance, a box containing only wooden beads (class B), most of them brown (class A), but two of them white (class A'). The child was then asked whether the box contained more wooden beads or more brown beads [p. 163]." Various techniques were employed to make certain that the children understood the question being posed. Piaget reports three developmental stages for this problem, which characterize children four years of age and older. During the first stage (until roughly six years), children assert that the brown beads are more numerous than the wooden ones. The reason they give is that there are only two white beads. According to the author, it is of no avail to point out to the children that the brown beads are themselves wooden. The second stage is transitional between the first stage and true understanding of the principle. Children in this stage may initially solve the problem, asserting that $B > A$, but revert back to the wrong answer when class A is made larger and larger relative to A'. The paradigm may be extended to a variety of stimulus materials.

The part-whole comparison task has provoked considerable interest in the possibility of training children who fail the task initially. This training question is of added interest because Piaget's equilibration theory (e.g., Piaget, 1957a, 1950b; Smedslund, 1961) implies definite limits to the efficacy of training procedures. Some investigators claim that training for this problem results in only marginal improvement (Morf, 1959), whereas others have claimed unqualified success in certain of their training efforts (Kohnstamm, 1963, 1967). Beilin (1971) reviews the controversy. See Inhelder and Sinclair (1969) for a recent Piagetian view of the training question.

Seriation of Sticks

Piaget (1965) gave subjects 10 sticks of varying lengths. The task was to order the sticks by length. The author reports that the youngest children were unable to order the series correctly. At a slightly later age, even if a child could order the sticks by length, he could not insert a new stick into the completed series. Variations of the paradigm are reported, in which other tasks are employed to investigate the children's understanding of ordinal number and its relation to cardinal number. Piaget (1965, p. 129) believes that preoperational children have difficulty seriating the sticks because the task requires considering a single stick as both longer than the sticks preceding it, yet shorter than those following it (or vice versa). The ability to take both viewpoints is bound up with the Piagetian concept of *reversibility,* to be discussed later in this chapter.

Elkind (1964) reports a replication study of Piaget's findings. See also Siegel (1972) and Murray and Youniss (1968).

Transitivity of Length

Piaget et al. (1960) employed the following paradigm to investigate children's understanding of transitivity of length (i.e., the principle that if length A = length B, and length B = length C, then length A= length C; and similarly, for inequalities). The children were asked to build out of blocks a tower that was equal in height to a given tower. The tables on which the two towers were built were different distances from the floor, thereby making a purely perceptual estimate of the relative heights uncertain. The child thus had to find some way to compare the height of the given tower with the tower he was constructing. Piaget wanted to know whether children would use various measuring instruments available to them in an appropriate manner. If a child uses a third object (e.g., a ruler, or perhaps even another tower) to carry between the given tower and his own, then he has a rudimentary understanding of the transitivity of length. Piaget et al. (1960) report a number of preoperational strategies for comparing the heights of the towers before correct use of a measuring instrument. For example, young children often build their tower to the same visual level as the given one, ignoring the difference in height of the tables.

Braine (1959) has challenged the tower-paradigm used by Piaget and produced transitivity of inequalities in young children with a nonverbal technique. But Braine's paradigm itself has been criticized for allegedly failing to test genuine transtivity (Braine, 1964; Smedslund, 1963, 1965, 1966). Bryant and Trabasso (1970) have interesting new evidence on the problem.

2. SOME PIAGETIAN THEORY UNDERLYING THE TASKS DESCRIBED: THE GROUPING

These four problems are typical of the experimental paradigms used to investigate children's class-inclusion and length concepts. Piaget is not reluctant to search for theoretical constructions to help explain his experimental findings. We shall not attempt a full-scale explication of Piaget's complex theory (see Flavell, 1963; Furth, 1969, for such an exegesis). Instead, certain features of the theory will be highlighted.

The central principle of Piaget's theory is that intellectual processes, like other biological processes, tend toward a state of ever wider and more stable equilibrium. The equilibrium is wider in the sense of encompassing more interrelated ideas and phenomena (Piaget, 1957a, 1950b). Equilibrated thought can best be described by means of logico-algebraic models that Piaget has invented himself or borrowed from Bourbaki mathematicians. These models include mathematical groups and lattices, as well as the logical analog of the group, called the *grouping*. Such algebraic structures have certain formal properties, which Piaget believes reflect analogous properties of equilibrated cognition. For example, groups and groupings exhibit the property of "reversibility," i.e., the identity element can be reached from any element through its inverse. This property reflects the reversible nature of equilibrated thought (e.g., the starting point of a problem can be returned to in the mind no matter how far along one is into the solution). It is the logical model for "concrete operational" thought that interests us. Concrete operations are supposed to characterize children between 7 and 12 years of age, approximately. The model pertaining to this developmental era is the grouping (Piaget, 1942, 1949).

The grouping is defined in a number of places (Piaget, 1942, 1949, 1957b, 1950b, 1970b; Piaget & Inhelder, 1969). Unfortunately, the characterizations sometimes differ. In the following definition we abide by Piaget's (1942, 1970b) claim that groupings are closely analogous to mathematical groups, differing mainly because of the grouping law of special identity. Essentially our definition can be found in Piaget (1950b).

A grouping is a set of elements, M, and an operation, o, defined on $M \times M$ which enjoys the following five properties:

(1) *Closure:* If $x \in M$ (i.e., if x is a member of the set M), and $y \in M$, then $x \circ y \in M$. That is, the range of o is included in the set M so that combining two elements of M by use of o results in another element of M. A familiar analog of this property may be found in arithmetic addition: the sum of any two integers is always another integer. Addition here takes the place of the operation o.

(2) *Associativity:* For all $x, y, z \in M$, $(x \circ y) \circ z = x \circ (y \circ z)$. That is, it makes no difference which operation is performed first in a series of operations. The analogy from arithmetic is associativity of addition: For any three integers $x, y, z, x + (y + z) = (x + y) + z$. Groupings are not in general commutative, i.e., it is not generally true that $x \circ y = y \circ x$. In this respect groupings are different from addition within the integers.

(3) *Identity element:* One and only one element of M, called "e," has the property that for $x \in M$, $e \circ x = x$. That is, combination with the identity element leaves any element of M unchanged. For addition of integers, the integer 0 is the identity element, since for any integer x, $0 + x = x$.

(4) *Special identities:* For every element $x \neq e \in M$, there is an element $y \neq e$ such that $y \circ x = x$. The element y is not the same for every x; for if it were then $y = e$ since by point (3) above, e is unique. Here again groupings find no parallel in the addition of integers. In a major work on groupings, Piaget (1942) distinguishes two types of special identities. One is called "tautology," by which $x \circ x = x$. The other is called "resorp-

tion," by which $y \mathbf{o} x = x$, where $x \neq y$. These two properties may be exemplified by taking x and y to be classes such that $y \subseteq x$, and by taking $\mathbf{o}$ to be class union, U. In other places (e.g., Piaget, 1950b), resorption is not mentioned.

(5) *Reversibility:* For all $x \in M$, there exists a unique element y such that $x \mathbf{o} y = e$. Analogously in arithmetic, for any integer x, there is a unique number y such that $x + y = 0$. The number y is of course $-x$. The reversibility property was mentioned above.

Piaget believes that the abstract structure of the grouping is isomorphic to the intellectual processes of concrete operations. The formal description of the grouping bears on various logical domains (e.g., classes, length) depending on the interpretation given to the set M and the operation $\mathbf{o}$. For example, if the elements are interpreted to be relations between temporal durations, and the operation $\mathbf{o}$ is interpreted to combine these temporal objects, then the grouping structure is supposed to reflect processes underlying a mature understanding of time (Piaget, 1969a). Similarly, it is claimed, velocity, classes, matrices, distance, etc., can all be captured by appropriate interpretation of the grouping set M and operation $\mathbf{o}$.

Two large categories of these different interpretations of the abstract grouping may be distinguished within Piagetian theory. There are "logical" groupings that deal with discrete objects that retain all their physical properties throughout operations on them, and there are "infralogical" groupings that deal with elements of a continuous nature whose physical properties are transformed when they are operated upon. The former groupings concern logico-arithmetic concepts such as class and relation. The latter concern physical concepts such as space and movement (Piaget, 1950b; Piaget & Inhelder, 1967). Moreover, coordination of different logical groupings underlies the child's conception of number (Piaget, 1965), whereas coordination of different infralogical groupings underlies the child's conception of measurement (Piaget & Inhelder, 1967; Piaget et al., 1960). The groupings involved in the experiments described in the first section of this chapter are the logical groupings for addition of classes and addition of asymmetrical relations. Infralogical groupings seem also to be involved in the transitivity of length experiments, since transitivity is fundamental to the development of measurement.

The logical groupings can be further subdivided according to whether they deal with classes or relations, addition or multiplication, and symmetry or asymmetry—a total of eight different logical groupings (Piaget, 1957b). The first two experiments described in section 1 concern the additive, asymmetrical grouping of classes (known as grouping I). The second two experiments concern the additive, asymmetrical, grouping of relations (grouping V).

The infralogical groupings may also be further distinguished according to an eight-way classification analogous to that for logical groupings. The classification is complicated, however, by additional distinctions among infralogical realms (topological, projective, euclidean; c.f., Piaget & Inhelder, 1967). Since our interest in this volume is with logical rather than infralogical thought, we shall not pursue the classification of infralogical groupings.

3. DIFFICULTIES ASSOCIATED WITH THE GROUPING

However novel Piaget's approach to cognitive development, his grouping model is unsatisfactory. Some of the difficulties are as follows.

The abstract grouping bears on different logical realms only insofar as the set M and operation o are interpreted to deal with them. But unfortunately Piaget is ambivalent about the members of the set M. Sometimes he states explicitly that they are themselves relational statements, such as $(A + A' = B)$ or $(B - A = A')$, where B is a set partitioned by subsets A and A' (Piaget, 1942). The operation o of the abstract grouping (not to be confused with the various operations occurring within the statements serving as elements of M) combines these complex elements according to a set of rules appended to the grouping postulates. See Flavell (1963) for a description of composition for different interpretations of the grouping when the members of M are construed to be relational statements. The difficulty with such an M is that the composition rules for particular groupings become excessively complex and *ad hoc* (c.f., Piaget, 1942). Elsewhere the elements of M, it seems, are considered to be simpler objects like classes, B, A, A', or distances (Piaget, 1950b, 1957b, 1970b; Piaget & Inhelder, 1969). But for reversibility to hold, having this M requires either (*a*) positing objects like class complements and negative distances, or else (*b*) introducing a second operation o' that "uncombines" what o combines (this is apparently the course taken in later works). There are problems associated with each alternative. Choice (*a*) causes closure to break down since $x \ o \ -y$ is not always defined in Piaget's system of eight logical groupings. In his 1949 statement (p. 93), Piaget accepts the consequence of no closure. But it results in considerable complication in stating the composition laws for different groupings. In other places (e.g., 1950b, 1970b) limitations on composition are not stated. One troublesome consequence of the absence of closure is that the grouping comes to look less and less like the mathematical group for which it was supposed to be the logical analog (Piaget, 1942, 1950b, 1970b). Mathematical groups enjoy complete closure.

Choice (*b*) is equally problematic. It is an abandonment of the grouping postulates. These specify only one operation. Nor would a new algebra of two operations bear much resemblance to the original grouping or to mathematical groups. One reason is that o' is not in general associative. For example, taking B to be a class partitioned by A and A', we see that $B - (A - A) \neq (B - A) - A$, since $B \neq A' - A$. Again, lack of associativity is countenanced in some places (Piaget, 1970b; Piaget & Inhelder, 1969) but not in others (Piaget, 1942, 1950b; perhaps Piaget, 1957b).

We shall not pause here to attempt the reconstruction of a

consistent statement regarding the interpretation of the grouping. That will be provided by an axiom system due to J. B. Grize (1960). Instead we turn to a related matter.

When evaluated only for its logical and mathematical contribution, Piaget's work on groupings has not been favorably received. Some of the problems that arise in translating the abstract grouping into statements about classes, lengths, etc. have been mentioned. Among professional logicians, reviews by Quine (1940), Beth (1950), McKinsey (1943), Kneale (1952), and Hempel (1960) are unanimous in finding Piaget's ideas obscure and often frankly in error.[1]

In defense of Piaget it might be said that the grouping model is part of a psychological theory. It is not promulgated for its formal, mathematical elegance. Indeed, Piaget (1963, p. 188) has been explicit in stating that the grouping model, as he enunciated it, is left largely unformalized. It was not until 1960 that the logician Jean-Blaise Grize first properly formalized the grouping according to the canons of mathematical logic.

However, even as an unformalized psychological theory, it is difficult to see the connection between Piaget's writings on groupings and the sort of data described in the first section of this chapter. We agree with Flavell (1963, Ch. 12) that few of the grouping laws are firmly grounded in evidence. Even Piaget's most thorough attempts at explanation by means of groupings are unconvincing. For example, solving the part-whole class-inclusion problem is assumed to require simultaneous apprehension of the equalities $(B = A + A')$ and $(B - A = A')$. The reversibility property of groupings is alleged to insure this insight for the mature subject. It is not made clear, however, how these equalities figure in the correct solution to the part-whole question (Kohnstamm, 1967, Ch. 1). Given the absence of rigorous data-prediction, the question also arises as to why

---

[1]Most of these reviews also touch on Piaget's logical system of adolescent "formal operations" (Inhelder & Piaget, 1958). Again, the comments are unfavorable. For a trenchant critique of Piaget's treatment of the logic of adolescent reasoning, see Parsons (1960). See Papert (1963) for a reply.

Piaget chose groupings as his example of reversibility, associativity, identity, etc. After all, one can envision numerous formal objects that can be plausibly said to embody those properties at the level of generality chosen by Piaget. Many of them will not resemble groupings in any obvious way.[2]

4. AXIOMATIZATION OF THE GROUPING

An axiomatization of the grouping provided by Grize (1960) is presented in Chapter 2. Grize's work injects clarity into any discussion of the empirical merits of the grouping. His formal characterization of it is clear. Equally important, the relation between his abstract grouping axioms and various interpretations of them into statements about classes, distances, and other logical domains is straightforward. The axiomatization allows many fundamental properties of classes, for example, to be stated directly, rather than as oblique consequences of the original five grouping postulates. An example of such a property of classes is the following: The same class added to two equal classes results in two new equal classes. This truth is a theorem of Grize's axiomatization (interpreted for classes), whereas it is difficult to derive from the original grouping postulates. What has not been provided is a rigorous psychological model based on Grize's axiomatization, and some experimental evidence bearing on the accuracy of that model. The present work attempts to supply both. The aim is to clarify the relation between Piagetian groupings and children's thought.

Although we shall be as informal as possible in this book, it may be well to treat axiom systems briefly. By an *axiomatization* or *axiom system* is meant the following: (*a*) a set of formulas (usually infinite) within which all "statements" of the system are made—this set of formulas is called the *object-language* of the axiomatization; (*b*) a subset of formulas of the

---

[2]Piaget's interest in the grouping probably stems in large part from his interests in "Genetic Epistemology" (see Chapter 11). The grouping is thought to be related to a mathematical group. The latter has an important place in the history of mathematics.

object language called *axioms* (or *postulates*); (*c*) rules of inference which justify deduction from the axioms; and (*d*) another subset (usually infinite) of the formulas of the object language called the *theorems* of the system. The theorems are all the deductive consequences (by the rules of inference) of the axioms. In virtually all axiomatizations, axioms are themselves theorems since they are trivial deductive consequences of themselves. However, for expositional reasons we shall use the term "theorem" to refer only to those consequences of the axioms that are not axioms themselves. The *theses* of the system refer to both the axioms and theorems, i.e., every formula provable from the axioms. In our terminology the theorems are all the theses except for the axioms. The theses of the axiom system constitute part of the system's object-language. On the other hand, the rules of inference are stated in the *metalanguage* of the system. In Grize's system, traditional logical inference is in the metalanguage. Thus, anything that follows logically from his axioms is a thesis of the axiomatization.

What is the relation of Grize's work to Piaget's developmental theory? The issue is quite complex, and discussion of it is postponed until chapter 11. Let us only make two points here. The first is that Grize's axiomatization has been fully endorsed by Piaget (e.g., Piaget, 1963, p. 188; 1967a, p. 83). In fact, it appeared in the series of monographs edited by Piaget called *Études d'Épistémologie Génétique*. Second, Grize designed his system to axiomatize all eight logical groupings at once (Grize, 1960, p. 71). (Whether it was meant to axiomatize the infralogical groupings is an open question.) Grize (1960) tries to prove this claim by means of a series of *metatheorems,* or statements *about* his axiomatic system. We shall return to Grize's claim in chapter 11. The different particular groupings result from different interpretations of the same primitive symbols appearing in Grize's axiomatization of the general grouping model. We shall show in chapter 5 how Grize's system may be interpreted to describe tasks testing children's knowledge of addition and subtraction of classes, and addition and subtraction of lengths. Be sure to observe, however, that Grize did not design his system explicitly for that purpose.

5. A THEORETICAL APPROACH BASED ON GRIZE'S AXIOMATIZATION

In this volume we present a theory of children's understanding of class-inclusion and length relations, and we report two experiments designed to test that theory. The theory is built around the axiomatization of the grouping provided by Grize. The delicate question of whether Piagetians are committed to believe that the theory is true is postponed until chapter 11. Grize's axiomatization is presented in chapter 2. The experiments are described in chapters 3 and 4. The relationship between the axiomatization and the experimental tasks is made explicit by means of *rules of coordination* in chapter 5. One of the coordination rules translates formulas from the object-language into tasks involving basic principles governing length; the other creates class-inclusion problems. Each coordination rule applies simultaneously to all the formulas in the object language (there is not a different rule for each formula). Chapters 6–10 are devoted to theoretical exposition coupled with analysis of the experimental data.

The experiments include a variety of length and class-inclusion tasks not seen before in the developmental literature. Of the four "classic" problems described in the first section of this chapter, only transitivity of length has an analog in the experiments to be reported.

2
GRIZE'S AXIOMATIZATION OF THE GROUPING

We shall reformulate Grize's axiomatization slightly to suit present purposes. The system will be described by relying on a set-theoretic predicate (see Stoll, 1963). In the ensuing discussion the traditional symbols of logic may be read as abbreviations for the usual English locutions. Thus, "if p then q" (for statements p and q) becomes "$p \rightarrow q$"; "p if and only if q" becomes "$p \leftrightarrow q$"; "p and q" becomes "p & q"; "p or q or both" becomes "$p \vee q$"; "not p" becomes "$-p$"; "x is identical to y" (for objects x and y) becomes "$x = y$"[1]; "everything has property P" becomes "$(\forall x)(Px)$"; "something has property P" becomes "$(\exists x)(Px)$."

1. AXIOMS

A *grouping* is a structure

$$(2.1) \quad \langle M, \leqslant, \leqslant_1, = , +, -, 0\rangle$$

where M is a set of at least two elements; $\leqslant, \leqslant_1$, and $=$ are binary relations on M; $+$ and $-$ are binary operations on M; and 0 is an element of M; all of which satisfy the following conditions (for all $x, y, z \in M$):[2]

---

[1]We shall use the sign "$=$" ambiguously. Sometimes, as here, it stands for the identity relation of Logic. Usually, as below, it stands for the congruence relation of the grouping. Context indicates which meaning obtains.

[2]The usual conventions govern the structure and internal grouping of formulas. See Appendix II for an explanation.

(2.2)   A1 $(x \leqslant y \,\&\, y \leqslant z) \rightarrow (x \leqslant z)$
    A2 $x + y = y + x$
    A3 $(x \leqslant y) \rightarrow (x + z \leqslant y + z)$
    A4 $(x \leqslant y) \rightarrow (x + y = y)$
    A5 $(y \leqslant x + z) \rightarrow (y - x \leqslant z)$
    A6 $y \leqslant x + (y - x)$
    A7 $(x + y = y) \rightarrow (x \leqslant y)$
    A8 $x \leqslant x$
    A9 $(x + y) + z = x + (y + z)$
    A10 $0 \leqslant x$
    A11 $(x = y) \leftrightarrow (x \leqslant y \,\&\, y \leqslant x)$
    A12 $(x \leqslant_1 y) \leftrightarrow (x \leqslant y \,\&\, x \neq y \,\&\, (\forall z)$
       $(x \leqslant z \,\&\, z \leqslant y) \rightarrow (x = z \vee z = y))$
    A13 $(x \leqslant_1 y) \rightarrow (x \leqslant y - (y - x))$
    A14 $(w \leqslant y) \rightarrow (w \in M)$
    A15 $(x \leqslant_1 y) \rightarrow (y - x \in M)$
    A16 $(x \leqslant_1 y) \rightarrow (x + (y - x) \in M)$

These conditions constitute the axioms of Grize's theory of groupings. We make some observations about the axioms. A1 expresses the transitivity of the grouping relation $\leqslant$. A2 states that addition is commutative. That addition is also associative is stated by A9. A4 and A7 could be written as one formula with a biconditional ($\leftrightarrow$) replacing the conditional ($\rightarrow$) sign. We have chosen to express it in two axioms because, for practical considerations of time, only one of the axioms, A4, was converted into tasks in the length and class-inclusion experiments. Together, A4 and A9 help give the axiom system its Boolean algebraic quality. In fact, as Piaget (1963) points out, Grize's system is in most respects a fragment of Boolean algebra. A8 indicates that the relation $\leqslant$ is reflexive. A10 says that 0 is the smallest element. A12 captures the notion of contiguity of elements; if x $\leqslant_1 y$ then x is the largest element that can stand in the relation $\leqslant$ to y and still be distinct from it. The occurence of the relation $\leqslant_1$ in the grouping structure arises from Grize's attempt to arrive at number from the groupings—though he is not trying to define numbers from groupings or actually to deduce their properties from the grouping axioms. In showing how the grouping axioms may be modified for numbers, Grize follows Piaget's (1942, 1965) analysis of the genesis of the concept of number in the child. The relation $\leqslant_1$ is of use in this pursuit since it enables the successor function to be defined. It also helps to capture, according to Grize, the dichotomy property of all groupings. Despite its importance, none of our tasks have investigated the relation $\leqslant_1$ in our subjects' thinking. For this reason we will have little to do with it in the sequel.

The numbering of the axioms has been determined in part by the decisions concerning which ones to interpret, via the coordination rules, into experimental tasks. Not all of the axioms could be tested.

2. SOME THEOREMS

The following formulas follow, as theorems, from the axioms. The theorems apply for all $w, x, y, z \in M$.

(2.3) T1 $(x = y \,\&\, y = z) \rightarrow (x = z)$
      T2 $(x = y) \rightarrow (x + z = y + z)$
      T3 $x + x = x$
      T4 $(x \leqslant z \,\&\, y \leqslant z) \rightarrow (x + y \leqslant z)$
      T5 $(x \leqslant y) \rightarrow (x - z \leqslant y - z)$
      T6 $(x \leqslant y) \rightarrow (z - y \leqslant z - x)$
      T7 $(w \leqslant x \,\&\, x + y \leqslant z) \rightarrow (w + y \leqslant z)$
      T8 $(x = y) \rightarrow (x - y = 0)$

The proofs of these theorems are simple. T1, for example, follows from A11 and A1. Grize derives T5 as follows.

(2.4) (a) $x \leqslant y$ (hypothesis)
      (b) $y \leqslant z + (y - z)$ (A6)
      (c) $x \leqslant z + (y - z)$ (a, b, A1)
      (d) $x - z \leqslant y - z$ (c, A5)

Proof of the other theorems is found in Appendix I.

Theorems T1–T8 are no more than representative of the infinite number of theorems derivable from the axioms of the grouping. The theorems in (2.3) were chosen for study on the informal grounds that they "looked interesting."

3. STATEMENTS THAT ARE NOT THEOREMS

A theorem of an axiom system is a formula that may be deduced from the axioms by means of the system's rules of inference; in our case, traditional logic. All the formulas that cannot be so deduced are not theorems. In chapter 6 the question of demonstrating the underivability of a formula from a set of axioms will arise. The question may be stated this way: Given a formula f, how can it be shown that f cannot be derived from the axioms of the system, A1–A16, by means of the rules of traditional logical inference? The answer is to produce a *particular* grouping in which the formula is false. This particular grouping results from some choice for the set M, relations, operations, and zero element of the abstract grouping. This particular grouping has the structure of (2.1) and is governed by axioms (2.2), but by virtue of its chosen relations, etc., the formula f is a falsehood. If such a grouping exists, then f cannot be derived from the axioms A1–A16. This method of demonstrating nontheoremhood works because the rules of inference of logic produce only true conclusions from true premises, regardless of the meaning of the propositions involved. Hence, if a grouping is exhibited such that the meaning of the elements of the structure makes the formula f false, the latter is not derivable by logic from the grouping's axioms. A more formal statement of this principle involves the concept of a "model" (in the logical sense); c.f., Suppes, (1957).

It can be easily shown that the following formulas are not theorems of Grize's system. For all x, y, z,

$$(2.5) \quad \text{(a)} \quad (x+y \leqslant z) \rightarrow (x+y \leqslant z-y)$$
$$(x \leqslant z) \rightarrow (x+y \leqslant z)$$
$$(x \leqslant y \ \& \ z \leqslant x+y) \rightarrow (x \leqslant z)$$

$$(x \leqslant y) \rightarrow (y - z \leqslant x)$$
$$(x + y \leqslant x + z) \rightarrow (z \leqslant x + y)$$
$$(x \leqslant y + z) \rightarrow (y + z \leqslant y + x)$$
$$(x \leqslant y + z) \rightarrow (y \leqslant z + x)$$
$$(x \leqslant y) \rightarrow (z + x \leqslant x + y)$$
$$(x \leqslant y + z) \rightarrow (x \leqslant y)$$
$$(x \leqslant y) \rightarrow (y - z \leqslant x + z)$$
$$(x \leqslant y \ \& \ x \leqslant z) \rightarrow (x + z \leqslant y)$$

(b) $(x \leqslant y) \rightarrow (y \leqslant x + z)$
$$(x \leqslant y + z) \rightarrow (z \leqslant x)$$
$$(x \leqslant y) \rightarrow (y - x \leqslant x + z)$$
$$(x \leqslant y) \rightarrow (x \leqslant y - z)$$
$$(x \leqslant y \ \& \ x \leqslant z) \rightarrow (x + z \leqslant y)$$
$$(x \leqslant z \ \& \ y \leqslant z) \rightarrow (z \leqslant x + y)$$
$$(x \leqslant y + z) \rightarrow (y \leqslant x + z)$$
$$(x \leqslant y) \rightarrow (y - z \leqslant x)$$

The proof consists in interpreting the grouping structure (2.1) as the structure shown in (2.6), where $P(X)$ is the set of all subsets of the nonempty set X (the "power set" of X), $x \leqslant y$ if and only if $x \subseteq y$ (x is included in y), $x \leqslant_1 y$ if and only if $x \subseteq_1 y$ ($y \sim x$ is a unit set), $x = y$ if and only if $x \equiv y$ (x and y have the same members), $x + y = x \cup y$ (the union of x and y), $x - y = x \sim y$ (the difference of x and y), and $0 = \emptyset$ (the null set). It may be verified

(2.6) $\langle P(X), \subseteq, \subseteq_1, \equiv, +, -, \emptyset \rangle$

that the axioms (2.2) are true statements when interpreted this way. Moreover, since our rules of inference give only true conclusions from true premises, all of the theorems of axioms (2.2) are also true for the structure (2.6). The reader may verify this for theorems (2.3). But the formulas in (2.5) turn out to be false in the grouping (2.6). Hence they are not theorems of groupings. In chapters 3 and 4 the formulas of (2.5) will be seen to represent class-inclusion and length tasks without solution.

An interesting category of formulas that are not theorems of Grize's axioms are those which are nonetheless true in certain Boolean algebras. It is uncertain whether there are any such formulas. A likely candidate is formula (2.7), where $x \odot y = (x + y) - [(x - y) + (y - x)]$, and $x \oplus y = x + y$. The present writer has been unable either to deduce (2.7)

$$(2.7) \quad x \odot (y \oplus z) = (x \odot y) \oplus (x \odot z)$$

from the axioms (2.2), or to devise a grouping in which (2.7) is false (and hence not a theorem). Formula (2.7) may be interpreted as one of the formulas of distributivity in the class algebra of all subsets of a set. Hence, if (2.7) is in fact not derivable, then Grize's axioms do not completely describe the truths of classes as specified in a Boolean algebra. We may then call Grize's system "incomplete for class algebra" (for a discussion of the various important notions of incompleteness, see Stoll, 1963).

Whether Grize's system is incomplete for class algebra is thus not certain, although Piaget's (1963) remark that the system is only a fragment of Boolean algebra indicates that it is in fact incomplete. Such incompleteness is not necessarily a flaw in Grize's system, given his goal of axiomatizing the grouping. The grouping is supposed to be a model of not yet fully mature logical thought. Indeed, Inhelder and Piaget (1958) claim that the full algebra of logic and classes must wait for "formal operations," which begin around puberty.

Another possible type of nontheorem is the formula that is not well-formed for Grize's system. These might include a formula which represents a truth about some logical domain within an alternative system, a truth which cannot be expressed by a well-formed formula of Grize's system. A possible example is the law of double negation, expressed as formula (2.8).

$$(2.8) \quad (\alpha')' = \alpha$$

Interpreted for classes, (2.8) says that the complement of the complement of a class is that class again.

It seems likely that Grize's system cannot express this fact about classes for want of a one-place operation that functions like complementation, and for want of the analog of a "universal set." If the proposition expressed by (2.8) is not expressible by a well-formed formula of Grize's system, then, following Copi (1967, section 6.4), we may say that Grize's system is not *expressively complete* for the logic of classes. As with completeness for the class-algebra, Grize's system is not necessarily to be criticized for lack of expressive completeness, given his aim of formalizing a model of immature logical thought.

3
THE LENGTH EXPERIMENT

1. DESIGN RATIONALE

The experiment's major objective was to determine the subjects' understanding of various principles concerning length that were embodied in Grize's axiom system. To this end, 14 tasks instancing those principles as length problems were administered to the children. It was necessary, however, to control the children's tendency to guess in a problem that they could not solve inferentially. To limit guessing, 11 tasks that in fact were not solvable were randomly intermixed within the 14 solvable tasks. The subjects were warned repeatedly that some of the tasks had no answer, and that when they found such a task, the "best" thing to do was to say that not enough information was provided for the problem's solution. Explanations for their answers were also required in an attempt to make lucky guesses improbable.

2. SUBJECTS

First, second, and third graders from two suburban schools near Philadelphia served as subjects. The first graders came from one school, and the second and third graders came from the other. Thirty children were selected randomly from the classrooms, five of each sex from each grade. The sample included eight 6-year-olds (mean age 6 years, 9 months), eight 7-

year-olds (mean age 7 years, 7 months), ten 8-year-olds (mean age 8 years, 7 months), and four 9-year-olds (mean age 9 years, 4 months). The children came from middle class homes. All were Caucasian. No subjects were dropped.

3. APPARATUS

The subject sat before a wooden apparatus painted uniformly gray. It is diagrammed in Fig. 1. The apparatus included a 26" ×

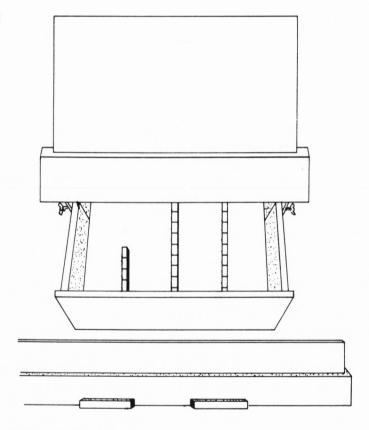

Fig. 1. Length experiment apparatus.

18″ board, one end of which was set on legs so as to incline it toward the child at 45°. At the foot of the board and at right angles to it, was a 3″ × 18″ wooden strip which served as a stage. The screen was placed to leave a 2½″ gap between it and the board underneath. Another, low, screen was placed in the front of the apparatus to insure that the subject viewed it from a downward angle. Long wooden sticks with ¾″-square cross sections could be inserted from behind the apparatus. The sticks came to rest along the board with their bottom ends touching the stage at the foot of the board. The tops were sometimes hidden by the screen, depending on the sticks' lengths. The sticks were of various colors and were marked off into 1½″ segments by horizontal black lines. This made visual comparison of lengths of sticks very easy.

4. DESIGN

Children were tested individually in four sessions spread out over 2–3 weeks. Session 1 was designed to (a) familiarize the child with the test materials and procedures of the length tasks administered in the following three sessions and (b) show the subject that not all questions that the experimenter might ask had answers. Sessions 2, 3, and 4 each began with an abbreviated version of the familiarization procedure of session 1. During the remainder of these three sessions each child took 25 tasks testing their understanding of length relations. Eleven of these tasks were insolvable. The order of presentation of the tasks was randomized for each subject, with the restriction that 5 or 6 of the insolvable tasks fell among the first 12 tasks, and the rest among the second 13 tasks. The plan was for 8 tasks to be administered in each of the second and third sessions, and 9 tasks during the last session. But in practice, individual differences in the children and in the tasks resulted in deviations from that routine. Each session took 20–30 minutes. The children were told that the experimenter had "games" to play with them, and almost all enjoyed the sessions.

5. PROCEDURE: Session 1

Familiarization

E explained the "rules of the game" to *S*. A number of sticks were placed in the apparatus before the child, and the screen was removed so that the entire extent of the sticks was visible. *E* said that the game they would play would use sticks like the sample ones. *S* then named the colors. It was explained that in the game *E* would ask *S* whether different sticks were the same length or whether one was longer than another. To illustrate, *S* was asked to make three or four relative-length judgments between pairs of sticks. These judgments presented no difficulty due to the large, regular, differences between sticks of different sizes. It was explained that during the games *E* was allowed to do three things to the sticks. These operations were as follows.

Addition.[1] Two sticks were *added* by concatenating one to the top of another so that the length of the result was the sum of the lengths of the component sticks. This process is schematized in Fig. 2. The operation is performed slowly and in full view of the

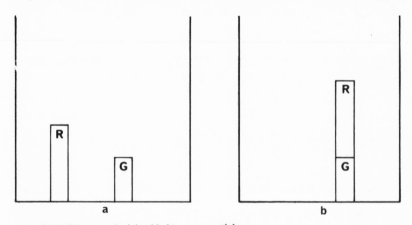

Fig. 2. Addition: a red stick added to a green stick.

[1]The subject was not asked to memorize the names of the operations, or even the operations themselves. The purpose of showing them to *S* during the first session was simply to familiarize him with procedures he would see in later problems.

subject. *E* illustrated this for *S* and then had *S* make relative length comparisons between two added sticks and single or other added sticks. If a blue and yellow stick were added and compared to a red stick, the questions were: "Which is longer, the blue and yellow sticks together, or the red stick? Which is shorter? Are the blue and yellow sticks together the same length as the red stick?"

Subtraction. A shorter stick was moved flush against a longer stick and the height of the shorter stick was marked off against the longer stick with *E*'s finger. Because of the equally-spaced intervals between the horizontal black lines on the sticks, the shorter stick always ended at a black line on the longer stick. To complete the subtraction, the length of the shorter stick was removed from the bottom of the longer stick. This was possible because the longer stick had previously been cut at the black line corresponding to the shorter stick's length. The remainder of the longer stick slid down the inclined board and hit the stage with an audible knock. The piece of the longer stick that had been subtracted was left on the stage. The subtraction operation is illustrated in Fig. 3. This manipulation of the sticks was always done slowly and in full view of the subject. After *E* illustrated the process a few times, *S* tried it once or twice for himself.

Stacking. Two sticks were stacked by slowly placing one in front of the other so that the interface between the sticks was one of the long rectangles along the side of the shorter stick.

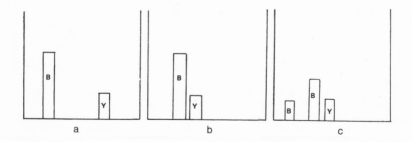

Fig. 3. Subtraction: a yellow stick subtracted from a blue stick.

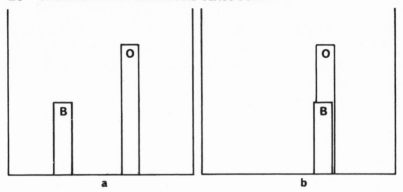

Fig. 4. Stacking: a blue stick stacked over an orange stick.

Stacking is illustrated in Fig. 4. *E* explained that the game only involved the length of sticks and never their thickness. Hence, the length of two stacked sticks is equal to the length of the longer stick. *S* was asked to show with his finger how long various combinations of stacked sticks were, and to compare their lengths against single sticks or other stacked pairs. Component sticks of a stacked pair remained discriminable after they were stacked, by observing the layers of the stacked combination.

The stacking operation must be distinguished from the addition operation. When the blue stick in Fig. 4 is stacked in front of the orange stick, the blue stick still touches the 3″ × 18″ stage. On the other hand, if the blue stick had been added to the orange stick, the blue stick would no longer touch the stage.

Undoing. There was a fourth operation, called "undoing," performed on sticks in the experiment. This operation was not shown to the subjects in the familiarization procedure, but it is described here because it will be referred to in later sections. Undoing is simply the inverse of addition: Two sticks of the same or different colors start off as added, and then the top or bottom stick is removed. The operation is illustrated in Fig. 2 if Fig. 2b is considered temporally prior to Fig. 2a.

The undoing operation must be distinguished from the subtraction operation. In the subtraction operation, one stick is used as a subtrahend to subtract a bottom piece of a unicolored stick. In the undoing operation, there is no subtrahend, the stick in question may be made up of different color sticks, and the top and bottom pieces of the stick are separated by removing either the bottom or the top piece.

Restrictions on Guessing

Finally, in session 1, E told S the "most important" rule of the game. During the game, the screen would be in place and S would not see the whole length of every stick. This was illustrated. Instead of just looking at the sticks, S would have to "figure out" which sticks were longer than which other sticks. The special thing about the game was that not every question had an answer. Sometimes, E said, S would not be told enough to figure out the answer to a question. In that case, S should realize that nobody could answer that question, not even S's teacher or parents. The important rule, E said, was not to guess. If S did not know the answer to a question he should tell E just that. In fact, for some of the tasks this would be the best answer of all. E illustrated this maxim by putting the screen in place and inserting two long sticks of different colors from the back of the apparatus in such a way that S could not see their total length. S was given some irrelevant information and asked which was longer. Other examples were adduced as necessary, usually not more than three.

6. PROCEDURE: Sessions 2-4

In sessions 2–4 the tasks that comprised the experiment proper were administered. An abbreviated version of the familiarization procedure of the first session was repeated at the beginning of each session.

The format of each experimental task was as follows. Sticks were inserted into the apparatus in such a way that, when necessary, the total length of some sticks was not seen by S. S might then be given certain information about the relative length of the sticks (e.g., the red stick is longer than the blue stick) and one or more of the four operations adding, subtracting, stacking, and undoing might be performed while S watched. The sticks were then restored to their initial state, and S was asked to recall the antecedent information, if any, and the subsequent operations on the sticks, if any. If S could not do this accurately, E repeated the procedure and S tried again. This cycle was repeated as many times as necessary. Most subjects needed only one presentation of a task for its proper recall. Rarely were as many as three presentations required. S was then asked about the relative length of two of the sticks in the apparatus, both sticks being partially hidden by the screen. Whereas the antecedent information was always given in the form of "longer than" (or "same length as") statements, the questions were always asked in the form of "shorter than" (or "same length as") statements. The reversal of the comparative from "longer than" in the antecedent information to "shorter than" in the question was meant to retard response perseveration. In all but one task, to be described, if X and Y were the sticks to be compared, the question always had three parts to it: "Is the X stick shorter than the Y stick? Is the Y stick shorter than the X stick? Are the X and Y sticks the same length?" All three parts of the question were always asked regardless of the subject's answer to any one of them. If the child answered the questions by claiming that not enough information had been given him, no explanation of his answer was required.[2] If he affirmed that one stick was shorter than, or the same length as, another stick, he was asked why he believed this. This was done whether or not S's belief was correct. Following his explanation, the subject was asked again for the antecedent information (if there was any). If he repeated it incorrectly (this rarely occurred) he was corrected and the task was repeated from the beginning.

---

[2]Pilot studies had revealed that explaining why sufficient information for solving a task is missing is rather difficult. There are many things that could be said to make a problem solvable, but none of it may be necessary for its solution.

Each task was performed with its own set of sticks. At the beginning of a task, sticks of the same color were always of the same length. The order of the three parts of the question—as regards whether the first, second, or third part required an affirmative answer—was counterbalanced across solvable tasks. Tasks with no solution required S to answer "not enough information" with no explanation needed; other answers to insolvable tasks were scored as failing.

For children who answered the three yes-no questions for solvable tasks correctly, explanations were scored as follows. Objectively, each of the solvable problems administered to the children was solvable because enough information was available to the child. Some of this information was simply given S by E in the form of antecedent information about relative stick lengths. Information about the operations performed on the stick was given by means of E's overt manipulation of the sticks, the sequence of manipulations being performed as often as required for S to memorize them (see above). In 11 of the tasks, however, a critical piece of information remained. This information was evident in the test materials in front of the child, e.g., some difference in the length of entirely visible sticks. For these 11 tasks, a child's explanation was scored as passing only if he invoked the critical information along with the relevant antecedent information given by E for that task. In the remaining three tasks, everything logically necessary for their solution had been provided by E in the antecedent information. There was nothing else in the test materials for S to utilize. In these cases, S had to invoke the information given him and withstand a mild countersuggestion from E (e.g., "Are you sure?").

A child was scored as passing a task only if he answered the comparison questions correctly and also gave an adequate explanation. E permitted himself to prompt a child, if an insufficient explanation or no explanation was forthcoming, by asking whether S "couldn't think of anything else." No other sort of prompting was given. Scoring the explanations proved easy. There was 95% agreement between two scorers for a sample drawn equally from all tasks, the sample comprising two-thirds of all the task protocols. Occasional difficulty arose for the two tasks involving stacking (see below, LA4 and LT3) which yielded only 70% and 80% agreement, respectively. Discrepant judgments were resolved by consensus. Subjects were not told whether their answers were correct. Instead, after each task, *E* said something like "All right, let's try this one now." It should be emphasized that a correct explanation was only part of the requirement for passing a task. As described, the child first had to answer correctly the question concerning the relative lengths of sticks.

We now describe each of the 14 solvable experimental tasks. The following notation will be used. The first letter in the name of the task will be an L, as a reminder that the task involved length rather than classes. If the second letter is an A, the task exemplifies one of the axioms of Grize's system (via the coordination rule). If the second letter is a T, the task exemplifies a (nonaxiomatic) theorem.

To facilitate exposition, diagrams like Fig. 5 will be employed. The figure represents a front view of the inclined board, but with the tilt disregarded. The thin rectangles represent the sticks. The letter in each one gives its color. The equally-spaced black horizontal lines have been omitted. The portion above the upper horizontal line represents the part of the board and sticks the subject cannot see. The dotted continuations of the rectangles represent the invisible portion of those sticks. For each diagram the reader should observe the differences in height of those rec-

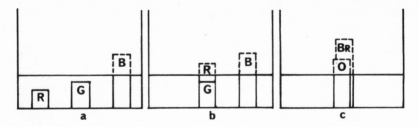

Fig. 5. Front view of inclined board with tilt disregarded. Addition is exemplified in a and b; stacking, in c. See text for further explanation.

tangles whose tops are hidden by the screen. The differences in lengths of entirely visible sticks were obvious in the task, and they were not pointed out by E; neither will they be pointed out in the description of the task. Similarly, the description will not mention whether a stick, before or after it has been operated upon, is entirely or only partially visible, since this is also evident from the diagram. The operation of addition is exemplified by Fig. 5a and 5b. The red stick has been placed on top of the green stick. The resulting stick is labelled G + R (the last letter standing for the stick that has been placed on top). Note that the green stick and red stick together extend past the screen. The result is that all of the green stick is still visible, but part of the red stick is lost from view. Stacking is represented in Fig. 5c. It shows a shorter orange stick stacked in front of a longer brown stick, neither of which is entirely visible. As a final abbreviation of the description of the tasks, we shall give only the first part of the three-part comparison question.

Before each task description the corresponding formula and formula number from Grize's axiomatization are given. The reader should be able to see the main correspondences established by the coordination rule by comparing tasks with their formulas, and by noting the following rules. The expression "$x + x$" refers to the stacking of one of the x-sticks in front of the other. The expression "$x + y$" (x and y distinct) is governed by two conventions. If the formula in which the expression occurs also contains the expression "$x \leqslant y$" (or "$y \leqslant x$"), then "$x + y$" means that the x-stick is stacked in front of the y-stick (or vice versa). In all other cases, "$x + y$" refers to the concatenation of stick y to the end of stick x, i.e., to addition. The expression "$x - y$" refers to the subtraction of the length of stick y from stick x. A final convention is required for tasks such as LT4. If two sticks x and y are related by $\leqslant$ to the same stick z, then the sticks x and y must be parts of a stick whose length is equivalent to that of z.

$$\text{LA1.} \quad (x \leqslant y \,\&\, y \leqslant z) \rightarrow (x \leqslant z).$$

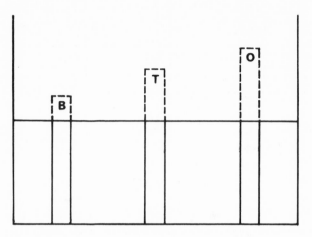

Fig. 6. LA1

S was told that the tan stick is longer than the blue stick, and that the orange stick is longer than the tan stick. (Fig. 6). E asked: "Is the blue stick shorter than the orange stick?" This task is one of the three in which no information beyond what is said by E is available from the display itself. Hence, instead of an explanation, S had to resist E's countersuggestion.

LA2. $x + y = y + x$.

S was given no information by E. He could see for himself that the two red sticks are the same length and that the two tan sticks are the same length (Figure 7a). E added one of the tan sticks to one of the red sticks, and the other red stick to the other tan stick (Fig. 7b). E asked: "Are the tan and red sticks together over here (indicating the left combination) shorter than the red and tan sticks over here (on the right)?" The critical feature of the explanation was that the red sticks were of equal length and that the tan sticks were of equal length.[3]

[3]The subject did not have to say that the order of addition was irrelevant, though some children offered this fact. If the order-proviso was made part of the criterion of a successful explanation we would have to ask why this irrelevancy is more important than other irrelevancies such as one combination being to the right of the other.

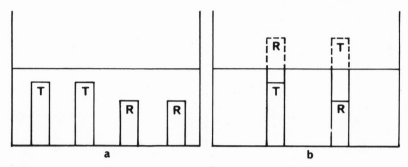

Fig. 7. LA2

LA3. $(x \leqslant y) \rightarrow (x + z \leqslant y + z)$.

S was told that the blue sticks are the same length (Fig. 8a). One blue stick was then added to the brown stick, and one to the red stick (Fig. 8b). *E* asked: "Are the red and blue sticks together over here shorter than the brown and blue sticks together over here?" The critical feature of the explanation was that the red stick was longer than the brown stick.

LA4. $(x \leqslant y) \rightarrow (x + y = y)$.

S was told that the brown sticks are the same length, and that the brown sticks are longer than the green stick (Fig. 9a). *E* then stacked the green stick in front of the brown stick (Fig. 9b). *E* asked: "Is the brown stick over here shorter than the brown stick with the green stick over here?" The critical part of the explanation was that the length of the stacked sticks was equal to

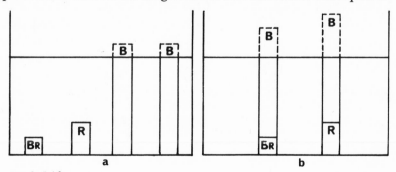

Fig. 8. LA3

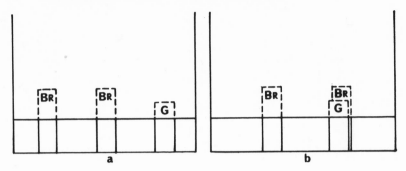

Fig. 9. LA4

the length of the longest stick, harking back to the familiarization procedure (e.g., "You just put it over the brown stick, the brown sticks are still the same *length* 'cause the green stick is shorter than the brown stick").

$$\text{LA5. } (x \leqslant y + z) \rightarrow (x - y \leqslant z).$$

S was told that the tan and blue sticks together are longer than the red stick (Fig. 10a). Then the tan stick was removed ("undone") from underneath the blue stick (which slid down the inclined board) and subtracted from the red stick (Fig. 10b). E asked: "Is this red stick (marked with a cross in Fig. 10b) shorter than this blue stick?" The critical feature of the explanation was that the tan stick was the same length as that part of the red stick that was subtracted (e.g., "You took the same thing from both sticks").

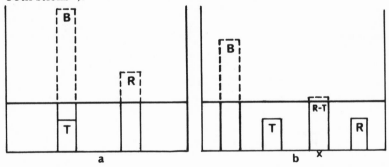

Fig. 10. LA5

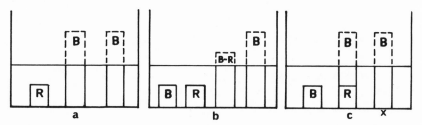

Fig. 11. LA6

$$LA6. \quad y \leqslant x + (y - x).$$

S was told that the blue sticks are the same length (Fig. 11a). The red stick was then subtracted from the leftmost blue stick (Fig. 11b). Then the part of the blue stick left over from the subtraction was added to the red stick (Fig. 11c). *E* asked: "Are the red and blue sticks together shorter than this blue stick over here (marked with a cross in Fig. 11c)?" The critical part of the explanation was that the red stick was the same length as the blue stick that was removed.

$$LT1. \quad (x = y \,\&\, y = z) \rightarrow (x = z).$$

S was told that the blue and green sticks are the same length, and the green and orange sticks are the same length (Fig. 12). No operations were performed. *E* asked: "Is the blue stick shorter than the orange stick?" This task is the second one in which no information is available from the display itself. Hence, besides relying on the antecedent information, *S* had to resist *E*'s countersuggestion.

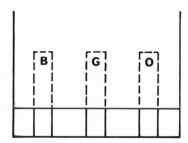

Fig. 12. LT1

LT2. $(x = y) \rightarrow (x + z = y + z)$.

S was told that the brown sticks are the same length (Fig. 13a). A brown stick was then added to the green stick, and a brown stick was added to the tan stick (Fig. 13b). E asked: "Are the brown and tan sticks together over here shorter than the brown and green sticks together over here?" The critical feature of the explanation was that the tan and green sticks were the same length.

LT3. $x + x = x$.

S was told that all three green sticks are the same length (Fig. 14a). One green stick was then stacked in front of another (Fig. 14b). E asked: "Is this green stick here shorter than these two green sticks over here?" The critical feature of the explanation was that the length of stacked sticks was equal to the length of the longest stick (e.g., "You just stacked them, that doesn't change their length").

LT4. $(x \leqslant z \,\&\, y \leqslant z) \rightarrow (x + y \leqslant z)$.

S was told that the blue stick and the green stick are the same length (Fig. 15a). A piece of the blue stick was taken from the bottom and left on one side, the remainder of the stick sliding

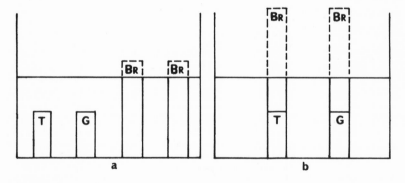

Fig. 13. LT2

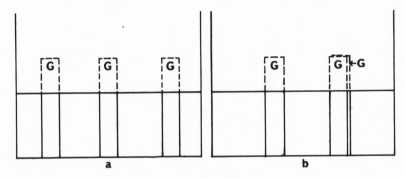

Fig. 14. LT3

down (Fig. 15b). Then another piece was taken from the same blue stick and added to the first part taken, the remainder again sliding down (Fig. 15c). *E* asked: "Is the green stick shorter than these two blue sticks together over here (marked with a cross in Fig. 15)?" The critical part of the explanation was that some of the blue stick from which the two pieces were taken to build the other blue stick still remained.

LT5. $(x \leqslant y) \rightarrow (x - z \leqslant y - z)$.

S was told that the tan stick is longer than the red stick (Fig. 16a). Then the orange stick was subtracted from the tan stick and then from the red stick (Fig. 16b). *E* asked: "Is this red stick shorter than this tan stick?" The critical part of the explanation was that the same length was subtracted from both the tan and red sticks.

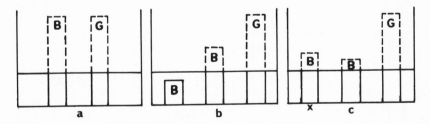

Fig. 15. LT4

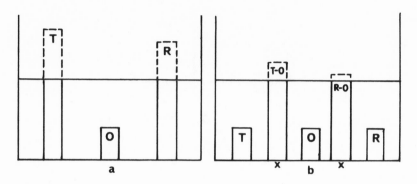

Fig. 16. LT5

$$\text{LT6. } (x \leqslant y) \to (z - y \leqslant z - x).$$

S was told that the orange sticks are the same length (Figure 17a). The blue stick was subtracted from one orange stick and the red stick from the other (Fig. 17b). *E* asked: "Is this orange stick (on the right) shorter than this orange stick (on the left)?" The critical part of the explanation was that the blue stick is longer than the red stick (hence, more was taken from the orange stick on the right than from the orange stick on the left).

$$\text{LT7. } (w \leqslant x \,\&\, x + y \leqslant z) \to (w + y \leqslant z).$$

S was told that the green stick is longer than the blue and orange sticks together (Fig. 18a). The orange stick was then

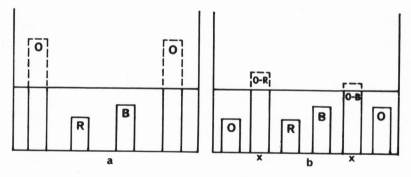

Fig. 17. LT6

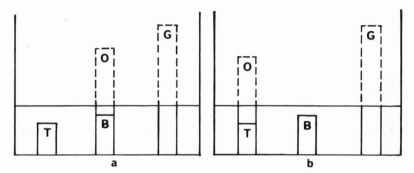

Fig. 18. LT7

removed from the blue stick and put on the top of the tan stick (Fig. 18b). E asked: "Are the tan and orange sticks together shorter than the green stick?" The critical part of the explanation was that the tan stick was shorter than the blue stick.

LT8. $(x = y) \rightarrow (x - y = 0)$.

S was first reminded how we "take away" the length of one stick from another by illustrating subtraction of the length of the green stick from the orange stick, both sticks being fully visible (Fig. 19). S was then told that the yellow and blue sticks were the same length. E asked: "If I take away the length of the yellow stick from the blue stick, how much blue stick will be left?" The subtraction was not actually performed. This is the third task without an operation performed on the sticks. To pass the explanation part of the question, S had to invoke the antecedent information and withstand a mild countersuggestion.

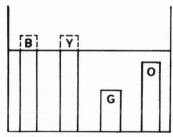

Fig. 19. LT8

The remaining 11 tasks are insolvable. Not enough clues are available from the antecedent information or from the visible part of the sticks themselves to infer the answer to the task's question. Hence, the correct answer was that not enough information had been given ("You didn't tell me enough"). No explanations were required.

The insolvable tasks follow from the formulas for nontheorems in (2.5a) by the same conventions that were applied for axiom and theorem tasks. Rather than enumerate all 11 insolvable tasks, we give one illustration. The nontheorem $(x \leqslant y) \rightarrow (y - z \leqslant x)$ becomes the following task.

S was told that the red stick was longer than the tan stick (Fig. 20a). The green stick was then subtracted from the red stick (Fib. 20b). E asked: "Is the tan stick shorter than the red stick?"

7. PRELIMINARY ANALYSIS OF THE RESULTS OF THE LENGTH EXPERIMENT

Table 1 gives the number of children passing each solvable task. The mean number of axiom-tasks passed per subject was 3.4 out of 6 with a standard deviation of 1.8. The mean number of theorem-tasks passed per subject was 3.8 out of 8, with a standard deviation of 2.1. The mean number of insolvable tasks passed per subject was 6.1 out of 11 with a standard deviation of 4.0.

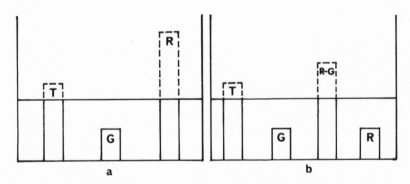

Fig. 20. An insolvable task.

TABLE 1

NUMBER OF CHILDREN PASSING EACH SOLVABLE LENGTH TASK

Task	Number of children passing the task	Proportion of children passing
LA1	15	.50
LA2	22	.73
LA3	23	.77
LA4	20	.67
LA5	6	.20
LA6	17	.57
Total	103	.57
LT1	22	.73
LT2	25	.80
LT3	21	.70
LT4	10	.33
LT5	12	.40
LT6	4	.13
LT7	11	.37
LT8	10	.33
Total	115	.48

The data will be further analyzed in Chapters 7–9. Four observations are worth making at this point. First, three children did not exercise the option of responding that not enough information was given to solve a task. These three children failed all the insolvable tasks. Nor did they mistakenly call a solvable task insolvable. Moreover, two of these children passed an appreciable number of the tasks that were logically solvable. The possibility arises, therefore, that these children managed to guess the correct answer and explanation to some of these tasks. One reason the insolvable tasks were included was to discourage guessing, and where they seem to have failed in this purpose we might be justified in disregarding the data from these children. However, the probability of guessing a correct answer and explanation seems so low (besides the difficulty of distinguishing the pure guesses from "educated" guesses), and the number of suspect passed tasks is so small, that it was decided not to exclude any subjects from the analyses to be reported later. Henceforth the insolvable tasks are not considered. Only the children's performance on the six axiom-tasks and eight theorem-tasks will be further analyzed.

Second, there were no striking sex differences. Consequently this variable will be ignored hereafter.

Third, no substantial learning seems to have taken place during the experiment. The number of length-tasks passed in the first half of the experiment did not differ significantly from the number passed in the second half.

Finally, Table 1 shows that the solvable tasks involving subtraction (or the similar operation of undoing) were more difficult than solvable tasks involving only addition and stacking. This result is reminiscent of studies showing the relative difficulty of negations and negative concepts (Bruner, Goodnow, & Austin, 1956; Wason, 1959, 1961; see also Wales & Grieve, 1969).

4
THE CLASS-INCLUSION EXPERIMENT

1. DESIGN RATIONALE

The major objective of the experiment was to see which of various principles concerning classes, embodied in Grize's axiom-system, the subjects understood. To this end 11 tasks exemplifying those principles as class-inclusion problems were prepared for the children. It was again necessary to control the children's tendency to try to guess the correct answer to a problem that they could not solve inferentially. To limit guessing, 8 insolvable tasks were randomly mixed with the 11 solvable tasks administered to each child. The formulas of these insolvable tasks are given in (2.5b) in section 3 of Chapter 2. The subjects were warned repeatedly that some of the tasks had no answers, and that when they found such a task, the "best" thing to do was to say that not enough information was provided for the problem's solution. Explanations for the children's answers were not scored. Instead, the same question was asked in different forms in order to make chance success on a task improbable.

The explanations were not scored, because in these problems there was nothing to justify an answer except the verbally given antecedent information. The conclusion simply follows logically. The reasoning process apparently is not open to introspection for our sample of children (nor, probably, for most adults). All the information required to solve the problem was presented verbally because it could not be presented in a perceptually obvious fashion (in contrast to the situation for the length tasks).

2. SUBJECTS

Second and third graders from one of the same suburban schools used in the length study, and first, second, and third graders from a Philadelphia summer camp served as subjects. Fifty-six children from these two sources were randomly selected for participation in the class-inclusion experiment. No subject participating in the length experiment participated in the class-inclusion experiment. One subject was dropped early in the procedure. Of the remaining 55 subjects, there were 22 females and 33 males. The sample included seventeen 6-year-olds (mean age 6 years, 7 months), twenty 7-year-olds (mean age 7 years, 8 months), ten 8-year-olds (mean age 8 years, 6 months), and eight 9-year-olds (mean age 9 years, 5 months). Subjects were middle-class Caucasians.

3. APPARATUS

The experiment involved a few dozen wooden blocks with average dimension $3'' \times 2'' \times \frac{3}{4}''$. A block could be any of four colors (blue, green, red, or yellow). A large black check, cross, or stripe was marked on the underside of each block. No block had more than one mark. The mark on a block could not be seen without turning it over. A cardboard shoe box for holding the blocks, and an opaque screen, were also employed.

4. DESIGN

Children were tested individually in four sessions spread over two weeks. As in the length experiment, session 1 was designed to (a) familiarize the child with the test materials and procedures of the class-inclusion tasks administered in the following three sessions and (b) show the child that not all questions E might ask had answers. Sessions 2, 3, and 4 each began with an abbreviated version of the familiarization procedure of session 1. During the remainder of these three sessions each child was given 12 or 13 tasks to test their understanding of inclusion relations.[1] These tasks were selected from a total of 18 tasks as follows: Each child took 5 tasks labelled CA1, CA3, CA4, CA5, CA6 described below. For reasons given later, we used no class-inclusion task that corresponded to LA2 (axiom 2). Each child took 3 or 4 of the 7 tasks labelled CT2, CT4–CT8. Note that there is no CT1 or CT3 (corresponding to LT1 and LT3). Finally, each child was given four of the eight insolvable tasks.

As just noted, every child was administered CA1, and CA3–CA6. Assignments were made randomly to determine which three or four of the other solvable tasks (all based on theorems) a child was given, as well as which four of the insolvable tasks he faced. The plan was to restrict the random draw so that equal numbers of each insolvable task, and also of tasks CT2, CT4–CT8 were administered across the subjects. Unfortunately, the experiment ended slightly prematurely, resulting in unequal N's for the tasks. The 12 or 13 tasks each child attempted were broken up as evenly as possible among sessions 2–4 and administered in random order. Each session took 20–30 minutes. The children were told that the experimenter had "games" to play with them. Almost all enjoyed the sessions.

5. PROCEDURE: Session 1

E placed between herself and S fifteen to twenty blocks. S identified the colors and shapes of the blocks. The marks were then revealed and identified. E explained that the same block may be called by different names, e.g., one block may be both red and square and also have a check underneath it. S practiced characterizing blocks by these three attributes. E then asked a

---

[1]The reason that fewer class-inclusion tasks were administered than length tasks was because they took longer. In order to have comparable diversity of inclusion tasks, not every task prepared was given to every child. See directly below in the text.

number of questions such as the following: "Which are the red blocks? Touch all the red blocks. Is every square a red block? Is every red block a square?" Explanation and coaching were given as needed. *S* was then shown the cardboard shoe box. *E* explained that in the game she would hide some of the blocks in the box and *S* would have to "figure out" what sort of blocks were in the box, e.g., whether they were all green, or whether some of them had crosses under them. To help *S*, *E* would give clues. *E* also showed *S* a screen that would prevent him from seeing which blocks were being put into the box.

Finally, *E* gave the "most important" rule of the game. During the game *S* would be asked questions about what sorts of blocks had been put into the box. The special thing about the game was that not every question had an answer. *E*'s explanation of this principle was similar to that used in the length experiment. Illustrations were provided as needed.

6. PROCEDURE: Sessions 2–4

In the next three sessions, the tasks comprising the experiment proper were administered. An abbreviated version of the familiarization procedure was repeated at the beginning of each session.

The format of each experimental task was as follows. Twelve to fifteen blocks of various sizes, colors, and markings (depending on the task) were placed on the table between *E* and *S* in such a manner that the markings underneath were not revealed. The child might then be given information about the blocks (e.g., all red blocks have checks). With the screen in place, *E* would then place certain of the blocks into the box. *E* gave *S* information about what kinds of blocks were in the box, but the screen prevented *S* from seeing which particular blocks had been selected. *E* would say to *S*, for example, "I've put every red block into the box, and I've put nothing else but red blocks into the box," repeating and rephrasing the information as it seemed necessary. After the blocks were in the box, *S* was asked to recall

all the antecedent information, if any, about the blocks and to recall which blocks E told him had been placed into the box. If S could not do this accurately, E repeated the procedure and S tried again. This cycle was repeated as many times as necessary. Seldom were as many as three cycles needed. S was then questioned about the contents of the box (e.g., "Is every crossed block in the box? Are there any crossed blocks left behind the screen?"). Regardless of his answer, S was again asked to recall all the information given him by E (if any). If he repeated it incorrectly (rarely) he was corrected and the task was repeated from the beginning. After this first question was answered, and the antecedent information was successfully repeated, a second question was then posed to further assess the subject's understanding (e.g., "Could there be a striped block in the box?"). Then, with the screen in place, the blocks were removed from the box and replaced on the table so that the markings were concealed. The screen was then removed, and E repeated the same antecedent information given previously. With the screen back in place, another class of blocks was placed in the box and S was informed about its properties. Again, the given-information cycle took place as above, and two more questions were posed using the same procedure as with the first two.

In all, four questions were associated with each task. The first and third questions were of a general nature (e.g., "Are all the red blocks in the box?"). The second and fourth questions were specific (e.g., "Could there be a square block in the box?"). The "specific" questions were picked to test the subject's understanding of the generalities. If the task had a solution, both general questions usually required affirmative answers (to their initial clause); the only exception occurs in task CT8. The correct answers to the specific questions were sometimes affirmative, sometimes negative, the selection being random. A subject was scored as passing only if he correctly answered all four questions. After the first and third questions, if the subject answered Yes or No, he was asked to explain his answer. These explanations were not scored.

Tasks without solutions included at least two questions that required a reply of "not enough information." However, children were prone to answer these questions with a *"no"* when they meant to say "no, not necessarily." Hence, an answer of "no" was treated as a "not-enough-information" answer if S invoked only the possibility, during the explanation, rather than the certainty, of a counter-example to the assertion included in the question.[2] Except for this qualification, a subject passed an insolvable task only if he answered all four questions in the task correctly.

Subjects were not told if their answers on a task were correct. Instead, after each task, E said something like "All right, let's try this one now."

The blocks were changed for every task. Whenever reference was made to markings underneath the blocks, a small white card with that mark was given to the child for the remainder of the task to help him remember what mark was involved.

We now describe each of the 11 solvable experimental tasks. The following notation will be used. The first letter in the name of the task will be a C as a reminder that the task involved classes rather than length. If the second letter is an A, the task exemplifies an axiom of Grize's system. If the second letter is a T, the task exemplifies a theorem.

We shall omit from the description of the tasks the procedure of insuring that the child remembers the antecedent information. The specific questions 2 and 4 are omitted (these were generally much easier than questions 1 and 3). Mention of the screen is also omitted. The procedure of returning blocks to the table and recalling the antecedent information between questions 2 and 3 will be referred to simply as "replacement." E's questions (e.g., "Are all the red blocks in the box? Are there any red blocks left behind the screen?") will be abbreviated to

---

[2]A similar situation did not arise in the length experiment. Most children were willing to claim that E had not supplied enough information for length tasks. There is no ready explanation for this discrepancy in the two experiments.

"Are all the red blocks in the box?" Finally, E's statements that she has put, e.g., all the red blocks into the box, and that she has put only red blocks into the box, will be abbreviated to the statement that she has put all the red blocks into the box (leaving out the second clause).

Before each task description the corresponding formula and formula number from Grize's axiomatization is given. The reader should be able to see the main correspondences established by the coordination rule by comparing tasks with their formulas, and by noting the following rules. The interpretation of $x + y$ is a locution which treats the classes x and y together, for example, "the red and green blocks," or, where appropriate, "the red or green blocks."[3] The expression "$x - y$" is interpreted as the expression, e.g., "all the red blocks which are not square."

$$\text{CA1. } (x \leqslant y \,\&\, y \leqslant z) \rightarrow (x \leqslant z)$$

S was told that all the square blocks were green, and this evident fact was shown to him by pointing to each square block. S was also told that all the green blocks had checks under them.[4] E said that she was putting all the blocks that are square into the box. (Q1): Does every block in the box have a check on it? After replacement, E said that she was putting all the blocks with checks into the box. (Q3): Are all the square in the box?

$$\text{CA3. } (x \leqslant y) \rightarrow (x + z \leqslant y + z)$$

S was told that every red block was striped. E said that she was putting all the red and green blocks into the box. (Q1): Is every block in the box a striped one or a green one? After

---

[3]The union of two classes sometimes is expressed in natural language by means of "and" and sometimes by means of "or." For example, the members of the set of Red $\cup$ - Tall things can be described either as "all the things that are red or tall," or as "all the things that are red and all the things that are tall." The intersection of the red and tall classes might be rendered "all the tall, red things."

[4]Here, as in all the tasks, E would illustrate this fact by turning over one of the green blocks briefly so as to show its mark.

replacement, E said that she was putting all the striped blocks and green blocks into the box. (Q3): Are all the red and green blocks in the box?

$$\text{CA4.} \quad (x \leqslant y) \rightarrow (x + y = y)$$

S was told that every blue block was striped. E said that she was putting all the striped blocks into the box. (Q1): Are all the striped blocks and blue blocks in the box? Is every block in the box a striped one or a blue one?[5] After replacement, E said that she was putting every block which is blue or striped into the box. (Q3): Is every block in the box striped? Are all the striped blocks in the box?

$$\text{CA5.} \quad (x \leqslant y + z) \rightarrow (x - y \leqslant z)$$

S was told that all the green blocks were striped or checked. E said that she was putting all the green blocks which are not striped into the box. (Q1): Does every block in the box have a check? After replacement, E said that she was putting every checked block into the box. (Q3): Is every green block which is not striped in the box?

$$\text{CA6.} \quad y \leqslant x + (y - x)$$

S was given no antecedent information to begin with. He was, however, given a brief look at the blocks to convince him that there was nothing unusual about this task. E said that she was putting all the striped blocks and all the green blocks that were not striped into the box. (Q1): Is every green block in the box? After replacement, E said that she was putting all the green blocks into the box. (Q3): Is every block in the box a striped block or a green block without a stripe?

$$\text{CT2.} \quad (x = y) \rightarrow (x + z = y + z)$$

[5]Note that there are two questions being asked in Q1. Both replies had to be correct for the child to be considered as passing it. The same will apply for certain other tasks described below.

S was told that every green block was striped and that no other blocks had stripes; only the green did. (For further clarification it was sometimes added that all the green blocks were striped, and all the striped blocks were green.) *E* said that she was putting all the striped blocks and all the red blocks into the box. (Q1): Is every green block and every red block in the box? Is every block in the box red or green? After replacement, *E* said that she was putting all the green blocks and all the red blocks into the box. (Q3): Is every block in the box a red block or a striped block? Is every red block and striped block in the box?

$$\text{CT4. } (x \leqslant z \;\&\; y \leqslant z) \to (x + y \leqslant z)$$

S was told that every blue block was crossed, and every red block was crossed. *E* said that she was putting all the crossed blocks into the box. (Q1): Is every blue block and every red block in the box? After replacement, *E* said that she was putting all the blue blocks and red blocks into the box. (Q3): Does every block in the box have a cross?

$$\text{CT5. } (x \leqslant y) \to (x - z \leqslant y - z)$$

S was told that every yellow block was crossed. *E* said that she was putting all the crossed blocks which were not triangles into the box. (Q1): Is every yellow block which is not a triangle in the box? After replacement, *E* said that she was putting all the yellow blocks that are not triangles into the box. (Q3): Is every block in the box a crossed block which is not a triangle?

$$\text{CT6. } (x \leqslant y) \to (z - y \leqslant z - x)$$

S was told that all the blue blocks were checked. *E* said that she was putting all the triangles that were not checked into the box. (Q1): Is every block in the box a triangle that is not blue? After replacement *E* said that she was putting all the triangles that are not blue into the box. (Q3): Is every triangle which is not checked in the box?

$$\text{CT7. } (w \leqslant x \;\&\; x + y \leqslant z) \to (w + y \leqslant z)$$

S was told that all the red blocks were square, and this fact was shown to him block by block. S was told also that all the squares and all the triangles were checked. E said that she was putting all the checked blocks into the box. (Q1): Are all the red blocks and all the triangles in the box? After replacement, E said that she was putting all the red blocks and triangles into the box. (Q3): Is every block in the box checked?

CT8. $(x = y) \rightarrow (x - y = 0)$

S was told that all the blue blocks and no others were checked. Only blue blocks were checked. (For further clarification it was sometimes added that all the blue blocks were checked and all the checked blocks were blue.) E said that she was putting nothing at all into the box. (Q1): Is every blue block that is not checked in the box? After "replacement," E said that she was putting all the blue blocks that were not checked into the box. (Q3): Are there any blocks in the box?

The remaining eight tasks—of which each subject received a randomly assigned four—are insolvable. Not enough information was available to infer the answer to the tasks' questions. The insolvable tasks follow from the formulas for nontheorems in lines (2.5b) by the same conventions used for axiom- and theorem-tasks. We give one illustration. The nontheorem $(x \leqslant y + z) \rightarrow (z \leqslant x)$ becomes the following task.

S was told that all the squares were crossed or striped. E said that she was putting all the striped blocks into the box. (Q1): Is every block in the box square? After replacement E said that she was putting all the squares in the box. (Q3): Is every striped block in the box?

7. PRELIMINARY ANALYSIS OF THE RESULTS OF THE CLASS-INCLUSION EXPERIMENT

Table 2 gives the proportion of children passing each solvable task. The mean number of axiom-tasks passed per subject was 2.6 out of 5 with a standard deviation of 1.3. Either three or four

TABLE 2

PROPORTION OF CHILDREN PASSING EACH
SOLVABLE CLASS-INCLUSION TASK

Task	Number of children taking the task	Number of children passing the task	Proportion of children passing
CA1	55	38	.69
CA3	55	34	.62
CA4	55	36	.65
CA5	55	27	.49
CA6	55	9	.16
Total	275	144	.52
CT2	33	22	.67
CT4	33	25	.76
CT5	33	14	.42
CT6	33	9	.27
CT7	25	18	.72
CT8	33	7	.21
Total	190	95	.50

theorem-tasks were administered to each subject. The mean proportion of theorem-tasks passed per subject was .50, with a standard deviation of .32. The mean number of insolvable tasks passed per subject was 2.3 out of 4, with a standard deviation of 1.4.

The data will be further analyzed in Chapter 10. Four observations are worth making at this point. First, 6 of the 55 subjects failed all the insolvable tasks they took. As in the length experiment, it has been decided to keep the data of these six subjects for subsequent analysis, because the probability of guessing one's way through a task seems low. Each task had four questions, some of which had more than one part. Subjects' guesses were probably not a completely random process anyway.

Second, there were again no striking sex differences. Third, no substantial learning seems to have occurred during the experiment. The number of tasks passed in the first half of the experiment did not differ significantly from the number passed in the second half. Finally, Table 2 shows that tasks involving a negation-like operation (e.g., "all the yellow blocks that are not striped") were more difficult than the others. Comparably to the length experiment, this finding is reminiscent of related findings concerning negations and negative concepts.

5
THE COORDINATION RULES

1. TWO GENERAL CONSIDERATIONS

When interpreting an axiomatization such as Grize's, the symbols "→," "v," "&," and "–" usually need not be assigned a meaning. They are the general logical words used to describe the connections between the nonlogical words that refer to the test materials. However, since we are not describing a realm of knowledge (such as the logic of classes or distances) but rather a set of tasks given to test knowledge, we must decide how the logical symbols reflect features of the tasks.

Ideally, the semantic rule would be constructed as rigorously as possible. When it came to assembling a task from the formula and coordination rule, little would be left to intuition or common sense. However, nothing would be gained from a great deal of specificity in the construction of the present rules, given the numerous sources of experimental error in administering the tasks to children. We shall only explicate enough of a coordination rule to make reasonably unambiguous what a task should look like, given its representing formula. Much of the rule may be induced by comparing tasks with their formulas.

2. THE COORDINATION RULE FOR
THE LENGTH TASKS

First we stipulate that axioms A7–A16 are not interpreted. The reason for this decision is pragmatic. Considerations of time made it impossible to interpret all the axioms into tasks. Moreover, A8–A16 seemed to lead to tasks that were either confusingly trivial or else passable by virtually everyone. As for A7, a related principle was represented by A4 (c.f., Ch. 2, section 1). These uninterpreted axioms are still part of the system, however, since they may figure in the derivations of theorems.

The bulk of the semantic rule is realized by interpreting the primitive symbols found in the structure $<M, \leqslant, +, -, 0>$. We shall come to "$=$" presently. The other relation of the grouping structure, $\leqslant_1$, need not be interpreted because it figured in no task. We let M stand for a set of sticks of varying lengths and colors, all with a square cross-section and marked off with equispaced black lines. Such sticks were used in the length experiment. Different variables (e.g., x, y, z) in a formula are represented by a distinctly colored stick in a task.[1] Any one variable may be represented more than once by sticks of the same color, as the specific task requires.

The relation $\leqslant$ will have one of two meanings, depending on whether it comes before or after the logical sign $\rightarrow$ in a formula. If it precedes $\rightarrow$, then $x \leqslant y$ (or $x \leqslant y + z$, etc.) stands for information given to the child that the y-stick is longer than the x-stick. We thus ignore the symmetric part of the relation. If it occurs after $\rightarrow$, or if $\rightarrow$ does not occur, then $x \leqslant y$ stands for the three-part question described in section 6 of Chapter 3. These questions asked whether the x-stick was shorter than the y-stick, whether the y-stick was shorter than the x-stick, or whether the x-stick and y-stick were the same length.

How does the interpretation of $x \leqslant y$ affect the interpretation of $x = y$? Strictly speaking, axiom 11 demands that we give contradictory information to the child for $x = y$. This problem arises because we interpret $x \leqslant y$ as "y is longer than x" rather than "y is longer than or equal to x." The former formulation is

---

[1]Due to an oversight, the distinct-variable–distinct-color rule was violated in task LT4. Only two colors were used (see Ch. 3, section 6) instead of the required three. It is doubtful that this mistake made much difference to the ease of the task.

obviously easier for the children. Various maneuvers can rectify matters. We shall suppress axiom 11 for purposes of interpretation, leaving it only for derivations. Then the relation $x = y$ (when it precedes $\rightarrow$) is interpreted as information to the child that the x-stick and the y-stick are the same length; or (when it follows $\rightarrow$), as the same question used for $x \leqslant y$—but with a different reply by the subject counting as correct.

Had the relation $x \leqslant_1 y$ figured in any task, similar remarks would have applied to it, as for $x = y$. The relation ultimately would have been interpreted as the statement that the y-stick extends past the x-stick by one segment. For reasons of time, no tasks involving this relation were administered. Nor does any axiom containing this relation figure in the derivations of any theorem that is interpreted into a task.

The expressions "$x + x$" or "$y + y$" etc. refer to the stacking operation described in section 5 of Chapter 3. Otherwise, for distinct variables, the interpretation of "$x + y$" depends on context. If $x + y$ follows $x \leqslant y$ in a formula, then $x + y$ again means the stacking operation. If $x + y$ does not follow $x \leqslant y$, then the y-stick is added to the top of the x-stick, which was described earlier as the addition operation (Ch. 3, section 5).[2] Except when zero occurs (see below), the stacking and addition operations always precede any questions pertaining to $x - y$ or $x + y$, if any operations are to be carried out.

One more convention for $+$ needs stating. A difficulty may be seen in connection with theorem 4: If the coordination rule is followed as we have stated it, theorem 4 is not true for our sticks and apparatus. The reason is that $x \leqslant y$ was not originally meant to compare different lengths, but rather to symbolize something like "the length of x makes up part of the length of y," as if the stimuli were long, thin "Venn" diagrams. Then, the operation $+$ would always represent superposition of parts of the length.

---

[2]These conventions governing $x + y$ in various contexts are not entirely unambiguous, since the order of the expressions "$x + y$," "$x \leqslant y$," and "$\rightarrow$" in a formula should affect the interpretation of "$x + y$." Enough precision is achieved with the present formulation.

Theorem 4 presents no problems under this latter interpretation, but it is easier to design the other tasks using the interpretation we did. As a consequence, we must add the following convention to the coordination rule for length, in order to rationalize formulas like theorem 4: If two sticks, x and y, are related by $\leqslant$ to the same stick, z, then the sticks x and y must be parts of a stick whose length is equivalent to that of stick z. This last convention gives the task LT4 its particular character.[3]

The interpretation of $x - y$ is the subtraction operation described in Chapter 3, section 4. Again, the operation is carried out before any questions are asked regarding relations between the sticks, except when 0 occurs. The symbol "0" justifies asking about relations between sticks after describing operations to be performed on them, without actually carrying out those operations (c.f., task LT8).

The parentheses around terms in some of the formulas indicate which combinations of sticks are to be considered and manipulated as units. The logical sign "&" is interpreted as any of those English locutions used to conjoin propositions; similiarly for "v" and "–," were they to occur. Another consideration dealing with logic is that all statements are put into a logical form that maximizes the number of occurrences of the logical symbol "→." The universal quantifiers that are technically assumed to precede each formula are ignored for purposes of interpretation.

Each task is performed with the screen in such a position that the answers to the questions associated with $x \leqslant y$ and $x = y$ must be inferred (if the tasks are solvable) and not simply observed from the test materials. Correct answers to the questions are determined in an obvious way from the formula and task. In

---

[3] An alternative way to handle LT4 would be to stipulate that "$x + y$" refers to the stacking operation whenever x and y are part (including the entirety) of the same length. This convention covers the others for stacking as well. It was decided to utilize the interpretation given in the text because the resulting task LT4 captured a principle we thought interesting to investigate in the child: The whole length is at least as long as the sum of its parts.

particular, correctness of an answer naturally depends on whether the task is solvable.

With these conventions the length tasks of Chapter 3 can be reconstructed reasonably well. Just as importantly, any new formula not included among the theses listed in Chapter 2 may be interpreted into a new task.

3. THE COORDINATION RULE FOR THE CLASS-INCLUSION TASKS

Again we stipulate that axioms A7–A16 will not be interpreted for reasons similar to those stated above. In addition, axiom 2 will be left uninterpreted, because it did not result in an interesting task under the coordination rule for class-inclusion.

The bulk of the coordination rule is realized by interpreting the primitive symbols of the structure $\langle M, \leqslant, +, -, 0 \rangle$. The relation $=$ is treated shortly. No task's formula included the symbol "$\leqslant_1$." Time considerations were the reason again. We let M stand for subclasses of a set of wooden blocks varying on color, shape, and concealed marking. Such blocks were used in the class-inclusion experiment. Different variables (x, y, z) in a formula are represented by a distinct class, as defined by one of the attributes: color, shape, or marking. The extension of the classes may be identical, however.

The expression "$x \leqslant y$" (or $x \leqslant y + z$, etc.) will have one of two meanings depending on whether it is before or after the logical sign "$\rightarrow$" in a formula. If it is before $\rightarrow$ then $x \leqslant y$ stands for information given to the child that all the members of the class x are also members of the class y. If it occurs after $\rightarrow$ or if $\rightarrow$ does not occur, then $x \leqslant y$ stands for the four-part question seen in section 6 of Chapter 4.

Whenever $x \leqslant y$ was interpreted as information to the child, x was interpreted as a class attribute that is visible (color or shape) whereas the y-attribute was the invisible marking. We dignify this procedure by including it as part of the coordination rule. The reason for the specification is that children seem to have considerably more difficulty understanding the idea that an invisible class is included within a visible one than vice versa, at least for a discrete, finite, and concrete set of objects. When y is visible and x is invisible, "$x \leqslant y$" is usually interpreted as "$x = y$" instead. This fact was discovered in a previous exploratory study on children's understanding of class-inclusion with materials comparable to the present ones. A similar phenomenon is reported by Inhelder and Piaget (1964).

As with length, the relation $x = y$ is directly coordinated to the tasks (instead of via axiom 11). When the relation precedes $\rightarrow$ in a formula, the child is told, e.g., that all the red blocks have stripes, and no other block has a stripe; only the red ones do. For further clarification it is said that all the red blocks are striped and all the striped blocks are red. When it follows $\rightarrow$ the expression "$x = y$" results in the same kind of question associated with "$x \leqslant y$." Similarly, the interpretation of $x \leqslant_1 y$, were it to occur in a task's formula, would be that all the x-blocks are y blocks, and all the y-blocks *except one* are x-blocks. No formulas involving this relation were interpreted into class-inclusion tasks. The interpretation of $x + y$ is a locution that treats the classes x and y together, for example, "the red and green blocks," or where appropriate, "the red or green blocks." No qualification related to $x + y$ comparable to that discussed in connection with the coordination rule for length is needed. The expression "$x - y$" is interpreted, e.g., as the expression "all the red blocks that are not square." The symbol "0" justifies asking a subject if there are any blocks exemplifying a class operated upon by another class (c.f., task CT8). The parentheses around terms in some of the formulas indicate linguistic cues (stress, etc.) determining which combinations of classes of blocks are to be considered together. For example, $y + (x - z)$ is interpreted as, e.g., "all the red blocks, *and* all the square blocks which are not striped," while $(y + x) - z$ is interpreted as "all the red blocks and square blocks, *except for* the red and square blocks which are striped."

The conventions concerning logical signs are the same as for length. Each task is performed with the markings hidden and the screen in place, so that answers to the question associated with $x \leqslant y$ or $x = y$ must be inferred (if the task is solvable).

With these conventions, class-inclusion tasks such as those described in Chapter 4 may be constructed from the formulas representing these tasks.

6
THEORETICAL USE OF THE AXIOMATIZATION: GENERAL CONSIDERATIONS

1. AIMS OF THE MODEL

Grize's formalism will be the backbone of a model that attempts to explain children's understanding of the length and class-inclusion principles exemplified in the tasks of Chapters 3 and 4. How the formalism serves this purpose will be elucidated as we progress. For now, the following general characterization may be offered. By looking at purely logical relationships between formulas in Grize's system, we shall attempt to illuminate the *psycho*logical relationships between the abilities underlying the corresponding tasks. The merit of the model may be assessed by comparing its predictions about children's performance on the length and class-inclusion tasks with the children's actual performance. The model predicts the pattern of passes and failures of each child. It specifies which tasks each child will pass or fail, given that he has passed or failed other tasks. The model does not predict the absolute level of difficulty of tasks for any age level.

The theory developed here is meant to account for all the tasks specified by Grize's axioms in conjunction with the two coordination rules. This set of tasks is surprisingly large even for formulas shorter than specified numbers of symbols. The model will be tested with the much smaller set of tasks comprising the two experiments. If it is successful for these tasks, and for others from the larger set determined by the rules of coordination, we can then attempt to determine the class of coordination rules with which the axioms combine to give true predictions.

Our exposition of model and data analysis is organized as follows. First, the formal structure of the model is discussed in a general way in sections 2 and 3. Second, a naive version of the model as applied only to the length tasks is evaluated in light of the length experiment (Chapter 7). This first version is naive because it does not distinguish between what a child knows and what he actually can do in a given situation. Third, some theoretical apparatus based upon this latter distinction is developed to help predict the pattern of the children's passes and failures better than the naive theory. Again, the model is restricted to length tasks (Chapters 8 and 9). Fourth, the model is applied to class-inclusion tasks (Chapter 10). In Chapter 11 we take up the question of whether Piagetians would condone our use (or misuse) of Grize's work.

2. RELATIONSHIPS BETWEEN TASKS AND RELATIONSHIPS BETWEEN FORMULAS

Logical abilities (such as length and class-inclusion abilities) are like linguistic abilities in being generative. We have not been exposed to every logical truth that we in fact recognize as a truth. Examples of this truism are readily available. Somewhere in the nervous system is a finite set of processes that allow the construction of a much larger set of behaviors that psychologists call "logical." Without implying that they are spatially discrete (and in fact without implying anything physiological at all), these processes may be represented as in Fig. 21a. To simplify exposition, we assume only three such processes, labeled by Roman numerals. The horizontal line represents the boundary between what psychologists observe and what they must infer.

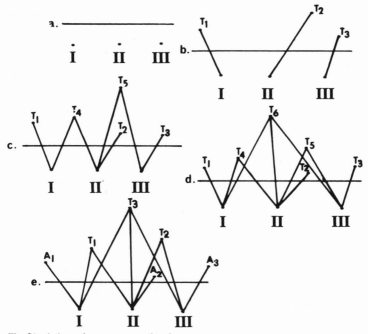

Fig. 21. Axiomatic-processes and tasks.

Suppose that each of these processes I, II, and III has a behavioral result, with no interactions among the processes. This result is successful performance on a logical problem. To some extent we need not *assume* that each process has a behavioral result unique to itself, since we may require this before calling such a process *one* process and not part of another. In Fig. 21b we represent these logical abilities as points above the horizontal line and connect them with other lines to their underlying processes. The labels T1, T2, and T3 stand for "(logical) task 1" etc.

Now suppose that two processes interacting with one another result in a new logical ability. This possibility allows a large number of abilities to be generated from a small set of representations in the nervous system. Figure 21c illustrates a new ability, T4, resulting from processes I and II; T5 represents one resulting from II and III. Thus there are five directly observable abilities, T1–T5, as well as three underlying processes, I–III, and seven assumed causal connections between the five observable abilities and the three unobservable processes.

If Fig. 21 were a faithful representation of some domain of logical knowledge, then a subject who has the ability to pass T1 and T2 should have the ability to pass T4. Likewise, being able to pass T2 and T3 implies being able to pass T5. The reasoning is this: If he passes T1 then underlying process I is in "working order"; if he passes T2 then the same is true of II; and if I and II are operating, then he can pass T4. Similar considerations apply to T2, T3, and T5. Conversely, being able to pass T4 implies that the subject will be able to pass T1 and T2, since passing T4 means that the subject has both I and II in working order, and these latter allow T1 and T2, respectively; similarly, again for T2, T3, and T5.

Finally, all three processes may interact, resulting in the logical ability T6 represented in Fig. 21d. By the same reasoning as before, being able to pass T1, T2, and T3 implies being able to pass T6, and conversely. But also, being able to pass T6 implies being able to pass T4 and T5, since passing T6 involves I, II, and III, which makes T4 and T5 possible. Conversely, being able to pass T4 and T5 implies being able to pass T6 by the same argument.

The place of an axiomatization in this scheme is perhaps already evident. We hope to find a formal system with coordination rules such that some of the purely logical relations between formulas parallel the causal connections between the tasks these formulas represent. In particular, we want the axioms of the formal system to represent abilities that result from only one underlying process. In Fig. 21b the abilities labeled T1, T2, and T3 are of this nature. On the other hand, (nonaxiomatic) theorems of the formal system should represent logical abilities resulting from one *or more* underlying process.[1]

---

[1] If more than one ability resulted from the same unique process, we could represent either of them as an axiom and the other as a theorem. This is why a theorem may represent a task with just one underlying process. Such a state of affairs is exemplified in the model constructed out of Grize's system.

Applying these ideas to the simplified situation represented by Fig. 21, we may relabel the tasks in terms of whether they result from interpreting axioms or theorems of the formalism. This has been done in Fig. 21e. It is important not to become confused by the new labels for the tasks. The points A1, A2, and A3 (above the line) are tasks resulting from interpreting axioms with a coordination rule. They are not the axioms themselves, which would make no sense. Neither are points I, II, or III (below the line) axioms. Instead, they are the elementary axiomatic processes (mental or physiological) which cause the abilities labeled above the line. Similarly, the points labeled T1, T2, and T3 are not themselves theorems, but rather tasks resulting from interpreting theorems. In summary, I–III are *axiomatic processes*. A1–A3 are *axiom-tasks*. T1–T3 are *theorem-tasks*. The formulas of Grize's system are axioms or theorems. Obviously, this system contains nothing called a "theorem-process."

3. A MORE FORMAL STATEMENT

The relationship between Grize's axiom system and the subject's observable behavior on a set of tasks may be represented more concisely. Let Th_i and Th_j be sets of theses that generate, through the coordination rule, corresponding sets of tasks T_i and T_j. Then we desire an axiom system in which statement (6.1) is true.

$$(6.1) \quad Th_i L \ Th_j \rightarrow T_i E T_j$$

L is the logical relation between sets of theses Th_i and Th_j which states that the axioms necessary and sufficient for the derivation of the theses in Th_i include those axioms necessary and sufficient for the derivation of the formulas in Th_j. E is the empirical relation between the sets of tasks in T_i and T_j which states that the ability to solve the tasks in T_i guarantees the ability to solve the tasks in T_j. All the examples discussed in connection with Fig. 21 may be seen to be special cases of requirement (6.1).[2]

4. SUBJECTS ON WHOM THE MODEL MAY BE TESTED

How can a theory of this kind be tested? Nothing will be learned if we test children too far along in development. If the children pass all or almost all of the tasks given them, it will be impossible to determine whether a child has passed a theorem-task because he has the relevant axiomatic processes—the latter being indexed by his performance on axiom-tasks or other theorem-tasks. If a child passes all the tasks we give him, any hypothesis we offer about the contingencies between tasks (an hypothesis due to an inferred intellectual organization) cannot be refuted by the data. For this reason, children who are not at an advanced level must be studied. These should be children for whom not all underlying axiomatic processes are fully operative. The model predicts that these children will pass specified tasks if (and sometimes only if) they pass other specified tasks. Appropriate training studies, of course, would furnish another source of predictions.

5. THE QUESTION OF NECESSARY AND SUFFICIENT AXIOMS FOR A THEOREM

Grize's axiomatization and the coordination rules of Chapter 5 will be used in a model of the type just described. Instead of positing only three axiomatic processes, the model posits about 16. Six of these result in logical abilities tested in the length experiment. Five were tested in the class-inclusion experiment. We shall simply assume the presence of the other, usually more or less trivial, logical abilities resulting from the other posited axiomatic processes. Whether this assumption is justified may

---

[2]A stronger theory than the one proposed here would require two-way implication in statement (6.1) where the present model has only one-way implication.

It may also be noted here that the model is subject to only a minimal amount of reaxiomatization, since most reaxiomatizations would shuffle the relations between axioms and theorems—resulting in very different predictions.

be determined in light of how well the theory performs in general.

In order to test the model we must determine the logical relations between axioms and theorems. It is a relatively simple matter to find sets of axioms sufficient for the derivation of each theorem. Derivations of our theorems T1–T8 are given in the Appendix. But to discover which axioms are *necessary* for the derivation of a particular theorem may be quite a complicated procedure. In general, one or more axioms of a set is necessary for the derivation of a theorem if the other axioms are logically independent of it. Apparently, in Grize's system, logical independence of a theorem from a particular subset of the axioms can only be demonstrated by constructing the appropriate grouping, according to the method described in section 3 of Chapter 2. Such a grouping is an interpretation of the primitives of the system such that the subset of axioms becomes a set of true propositions, whereas the theorem turns out false. If such a grouping can be discovered, then the theorem has been shown to be logically independent of that subset of axioms. The problem with this method of modeling (in the logician's sense) is that it lacks a *decision procedure*. A decision procedure would routinely guarantee the construction of the desired grouping, if it exists, and terminate in a finite number of steps if the desired grouping does not exist. No decision procedures seem available for showing the necessity of subsets of axioms for the derivation of theorems in Grize's system. Consequently, logical determination of necessary axioms may become a very time-consuming affair, with no assurance of success. Yet, theoretically, we need this information before our theory can be adequately tested. Our solution to this problem is not totally satisfactory. It takes as necessary and sufficient that subset of axioms that we can show to be sufficient for a theorem and within which there appears to be no smaller subset that is also sufficient for deriving the theorem.

This procedure is probably not too dangerous. The axiom-set seems uncomplicated enough so that the possibility of alter-

TABLE 3

NECESSARY AND SUFFICIENT AXIOMS FOR THEOREMS,
OF THOSE CONVERTED INTO TASKS

Theorem	Axioms
T1	A1
T2	A3
T3	A4
T4	A1, A2, A3, A4
T5	A1, A5, A6
T6	A1, A3, A5, A6
T7	A1, A3
T8	A1, A2, A3, A4, A5

native, minimally sufficient sets of axioms for a given theorem seems slight. However, if we call an axiom necessary, which in fact proves logically unnecessary, then the data analyses to be presented will need appropriate modification. Such modification would only be partial, because the claims about sufficiency of a subset of axioms will stand even if an alternative sufficient subset is found.[3] With these qualifications in mind, Table 3 was constructed. It shows the necessary and sufficient axioms for each theorem converted into a task, provided that those axioms were themselves converted into tasks.

[3]A model of the kind developed here will be none the worse if more than one subset of axioms imply a theorem. This model will simply make different predictions than a model with unique subsets such as ours, and experimentation will decide which model is nearer the truth.

7
THE MODEL FOR LENGTH TASKS

1. PREDICTIONS IN DETAIL

By applying the first coordination rule of Chapter 5, Eq. (6.1) may be converted into a model for children's understanding of length-relations. For each subject the model makes predictions based on Table 3. To illustrate these predictions, let us consider a certain subject of the length experiment. This child passed axiom-tasks LA1, LA2, LA3, LA4, and LA6. Table 3 shows that the model predicts that he will also pass LT1, LT2, LT3, LT4, and LT7. In contrast, the subject's failure on LA5 implies that he will fail LT5, LT6, and LT8: The lack of LA5 indicates that an axiomatic process necessary for these three theorem-tasks is not operating. In fact, this subject passed LT1, LT2, LT3, LT5, and LT7, and failed LT4, LT6, and LT8. Hence the model has so far made six correct predictions and two false ones.

The model has another source of predictions concerning the theorem-tasks which is independent of predictions made by means of axiom-tasks. Subjects' performance on one theorem-task may be predicted from their performance on other theorem-tasks. For example, since our illustrative subject passed task LT7, Table 3 shows that the axiomatic processes for tasks LT1 and LT2 are in working order. Hence, the theory predicts that this subject will pass those two theorem-tasks. By similar reasoning, success on LT1 and LT2 predicts success on LT7. The predictions go both ways in this last example, because the axioms for LT7, and for LT1 and LT2, are the same. On the other hand, Table 3 shows that our subject's success on task LT5 predicts success on LT1 but not vice versa.

We may construe the predictions of the theory another way, namely, as predicting failure on a task if another task requiring a subset of its axioms is failed. For example, if our illustrative subject had failed task LT1, we would predict failure on task LT5, since failure on LT1 theoretically implies lack of one of the axiomatic processes necessary for LT5. In contrast, the theory does not predict failure on LT5 simply because LT4 was failed. Table 3 shows that theorem 4 requires axioms not required by theorem 5. Hence, failure on the former theorem-task could be due to inoperative axiomatic processes unrelated to the latter.

These are the kinds of predictions made by the model as elaborated so far. Notice that we have not mentioned a perfectly valid kind of prediction which follows from the general statement (6.1). These omitted predictions result from the use of an axiom and theorem together to predict the presence or absence of another theorem. For example, since our subject passed LA3 and LT1, the model predicts that he will pass LT7. An analysis in terms of these sorts of predictions has not been carried out, in an effort to control a growing mass of detail; they are redundant with the other predictions in any event. Only the model's predictions from axioms to theorems, theorems to axioms, and theorems to other theorems have been analyzed.

How can we evaluate the theory's performance? For the moment we restrict ourselves to predicting which tasks will be passed rather than which tasks will be failed. First we list every passing-prediction of the model. For the particular theorems that were tested in the length experiment the predictions appear in Table 4. Although the same theorem-task is often predicted more than once from different antecedents, we count every statement in Table 4 as a separate prediction. This credits the theory twice if success on a task is predicted two ways and in fact occurs. Naturally, the theory is discredited twice if success on the

TABLE 4

PASSING PREDICTIONS OF THE MODEL FOR LENGTH

A. Axioms to Theorems

1. LA1 → LT1
2. LA3 → LT2
3. LA4 → LT3
4. LA1 & LA2 & LA3 & LA4 → LT4
5. LA1 & LA5 & LA6 → LT5
6. LA1 & LA3 & LA5 & LA6 → LT6
7. LA1 & LA3 → LT7
8. LA1 & LA2 & LA3 & LA4 & LA5 → LT8

B. Theorems to Axioms

9. LT1 → LA1
10. LT2 → LA3
11. LT3 → LA4
12. LT4 → LA1
13. LT4 → LA2
14. LT4 → LA3
15. LT4 → LA4
16. LT5 → LA1
17. LT5 → LA5
18. LT5 → LA6
19. LT6 → LA1
20. LT6 → LA3
21. LT6 → LA5
22. LT6 → LA6
23. LT7 → LA1
24. LT7 → LA3
25. LT8 → LA1
26. LT8 → LA2
27. LT8 → LA3
28. LT8 → LA4
29. LT8 → LA5

C. One Theorem to Another Theorem

30. LT7 → LT3
31. LT7 → LT1
32. LT4 → LT1
33. LT4 → LT2
34. LT4 → LT3
35. LT4 → LT7
36. LT6 → LT5
37. LT6 → LT7
38. LT6 → LT1
39. LT6 → LT2
40. LT8 → LT4
41. LT8 → LT7
42. LT8 → LT3
43. LT8 → LT2
44. LT8 → LT1
45. LT5 → LT1

D. Two Theorems to a Single Theorem

46. LT1 & LT2 → LT7
47. LT4 & LT5 → LT6
48. LT5 & LT7 → LT6
49. LT5 & LT8 → LT6
50. LT2 & LT6 → LT7
51. LT4 & LT5 → LT8
52. LT4 & LT6 → LT8

task is predicted twice and the task is failed. Using Table 4, we looked through the data subject by subject and counted the number of confirmed predictions. For each prediction, these were the cases where both the antecedent tasks and the consequent task were passed. We also counted the number of times the antecedent tasks were passed but the consequent task was failed. These gave the disconfirmed predictions. The proportion of correct predictions is the ratio of true predictions to the sum of the true and false predictions. Notice that not all of the predictions figuring in this ratio are mutually independent.

The outcome of this analysis is that the theory correctly predicts success on tasks 76% of the time, making 399 true predictions and 123 false predictions. This overall result may be broken down into predictions from axioms to theorems (1–8 of Table 4), from theorems to axioms (9–29), from one theorem to another theorem (30–45), and from two theorems to a single theorem (46–52).

When predicting from axioms to theorems, the model predicts correctly 81% of the time, making 77 true predictions and 18 false ones. When predicting from theorems to axioms the theory is correct 79% of the time, predicting correctly 182 times and wrongly 49 times. When predicting from one theorem to another theorem, the theory is correct 82% of the time, predicting correctly 115 times and wrongly 25 times. Finally, when predicting from more than one theorem to another theorem, the theory makes 25 true predictions and 31 false ones, for an accuracy of only 45%. There will be much said about this last outcome later. The results are summarized in Table 5.

To what extent is the theory confirmed by these results? Would less elaborate models perform just as well on these predictions? Before turning to these questions, the model's ability to predict what tasks a child will fail is examined.

The failing-predictions are simply the contrapositives of the passing-predictions. Thus from Table 4, since passing LT1 implies passing LA1, failing LA1 implies failing LT1. These two predictions of the theory are tautologically equivalent: If one of

TABLE 5

PERFORMANCE OF THE LENGTH MODEL:
PASSING-PREDICTIONS

Kinds of predictions	Number of true predictions	Number of false predictions	Total number of predictions	% of true predictions
Overall	399	123	522	76
Axioms to Theorems (predictions 1–8)	77	18	95	81
Theorems to Axioms (predictions 9–29)	182	49	231	79
One Theorem to Another Theorem (predictions 30–45)	115	25	140	82
Two Theorems to Another Theorem (predictions 46–52)	25	31	56	45

the statements characterizes children, the other must also. Just how this logical truth conforms to the logic of the model is easily seen. Consider the prediction that passing LT7 implies passing LT2. The prediction is based on the assumption that the axiomatic-processes for LT2 are a subset of the underlying processes of LT7. If LT7 is passed, then the axiomatic-processes for LT2 must be in working order also. The contrapositive of this law simply states that if the processes for LT2 are not all operable, which is inferred from the failure of LT2, then neither can all the processes necessary for LT7 be operable. The result is the prediction that LT7 will also be failed. In this sense the passing-predictions and failing-predictions of the theory are equivalent.

Despite the equivalence, the proportion of correct and incorrect individual predictions will nonetheless differ between passing- and failing-predictions because somewhat different subjects become involved in the testing of the predictions. To test the passing-predictions, only those children who have passed the antecedent-tasks from Table 4 are singled out. For failing-predictions, on the other hand, we single out children on the basis of their having failed the consequent-tasks of Table 4. True predictions then result from having failed the corresponding antecedent tasks; false predictions result from having passed them. The sets of children satisfying the initial clause of these two sorts of predictions will not necessarily coincide.

To understand the failing predictions it is important to note the effect of contraposition on a conditional with a conjunction in its antecedent. To illustrate, the failing-prediction that corresponds to the passing-prediction "LT1 & LT2→LT7" (number 46 in Table 4) is "fail LT7→fail LT1 or fail LT2." The difference between the passing- and failing-predictions makes sense in terms of our model. If the axiomatic processes indexed by LT1 and LT2 are sufficient for passing LT7, then if LT7 is failed one or the other of them (or both) must be absent, thereby leading to the failure of either LT1 or LT2 (or both).

All the contrapositives of Table 4 were included as failing predictions, except those corresponding to passing-predictions 1–8. These latter predictions complicate subsequent data analyses considerably. Moreover, little information is lost by the omitted analysis, since the equivalent passing-predictions were fully analyzed.

When the failing-predictions are tested against the data obtained in the length experiment, the theory predicts correctly 81% of the time, making 387 true predictions and 93 wrong ones. This result may be broken down as follows. When predicting what theorem-tasks the child will fail by seeing what axiom-tasks he fails (the contrapositives of predictions 9–29 in Table 4), the theory makes 108 true predictions and 37 false ones for an accuracy of 74%. When predicting what theorem-tasks he fails by seeing what other single theorem-tasks he fails (30–45), the theory makes 152 true predictions and 25 false ones for an accuracy of 86%. When predicting which pair of theorem-tasks one or both of which the child will fail by seeing what other single theorems he fails (46–52) the theory is 80% accurate, making 127 true predictions and 31 false ones.

In general, the model is at least as accurate for failing predictions as for passing-predictions. We shall next test the model against various hypothetical rival theories in order to better assess the model's accuracy. In the analyses to be reported, the model for failing predictions generally shows the same accuracy for failing-predictions as for passing-predictions. Consequently, we shall hereafter omit mention of the failing-predictions.

2. HOW GOOD IS THE MODEL?

We return to the question raised earlier. To what extent do these results confirm the theory? One first might ask whether the results just reviewed are significantly better than chance. But to answer such a question requires knowing the chance probability of a child's passing each of the solvable length-tasks. Since an explanation was required of the child, and since he always had the option of responding that not enough information had been given him, the probability of passing a given task by luck alone becomes inestimable. Instead of answering the first question, a different set of questions will be answered that are more interesting. We shall imagine four different theories, each of which perfectly predicts some aspect of the length experiment's results. We then ask how many of our model's predictions would be confirmed simply on the basis of what the imagined rival theory predicts. Does our model tell us more than the imagined rival about the pattern of passes and failures among the children? If not, then the present, rather complex model would be superfluous if that imagined theory existed. As a fifth test, we shall also construct an actual theory based on simple assumptions and assess its ability to predict the pattern of children's passes and failures against the ability of our model.

The First Rival Theory

For the first rival, imagine a theory that could accurately predict the probability over all thirty subjects of passing a theorem-task and also the probability of passing an axiom-task. The actual results of the length experiment, over all children and all theorem-tasks, were that 115 theorem-tasks out of 240 administered were passed. Hence, this imagined theory would tell us that the probability of passing a theorem task is 115 divided by 240 or .48. Similarly, the probability of passing an axiom-task is 103 divided by 180 or .57. Now consider the predictions of the model proceeding from passed axiom-tasks to passed theorem-tasks, i.e., predictions 1–8 in Table 4. Overall, 95 theorem-tasks were predicted to be passed by the subjects, on the basis of their individual performances on axiom-tasks. How many true predictions are accounted for by the imagined rival theory, which is oblivious to the alleged connection between axiom-tasks and theorem-tasks? Another way to state the question is: How many of the true predictions of our theory—from passed axiom-tasks to passed theorem-tasks—can be accounted for by the fact that the overall probability of passing a theorem-task is .48? The answer is the product of the number of theorem-tasks predicted to be passed by the real theory and the probability of passing a theorem-task, or 95.0 × .48 which equals 45.6. The number of false predictions that are expected from the rival theory is 95.0 − 45.6 or 49.4 (= 95 × (1.0 − .48)).

Thus, 45.6 out of 95 of our real model's predictions in this situation are predicted equally well by the rival model. Our model is more useful than the rival only if it is true more than 45.6 out of 95 times. Such an outcome would be evidence that the rival theory cannot account for the pattern of passes and failures as well as our model can. (Of course this would not show that our model is the best one possible.)

As reported in section 1, our model actually predicts correctly 77 times and incorrectly 18 times. This is much more accurate than the hypothetical rival. The logic of the procedure for the other kinds of predictions B–D shown in Table 4 (theorem-tasks to axiom-tasks, etc.) is the same. Overall, our model is 25% more accurate than the first rival. When the results were broken down into the four kinds of predictions A–D given in Table 4, it was found that the hypothetical rival is about as accurate as the real theory in predicting from two theorems to a single theorem (type D, 46–52). These are the same troublesome predictions of Table 5.

The Second Rival Theory

A more formidable rival theory can be imagined which predicts not only the probability of passing theorem- and axiom-tasks in general, but also the probability of passing each particular theorem- and axiom-task. For example, since 15 out of the 30 children passed task LA1 (see Table 1), the rival theory assigns a probability of .50 to passing that task. In the same way a probability is assigned to each task.

Now consider the predictions of our model proceeding from passed theorem-tasks to passed axiom-tasks (predictions 9–29 in Table 4). Over all subjects and all predictions of this kind, task LA1 should have been passed 68 times. The current rival theory thus receives credit for 68 × .50 or 34.0 correct predictions. The same analysis was carried out for the other five axiom-tasks and the results summed to give the number of true predictions of our model that follow equally well from the current rival model. This anlaysis thus answers the question: How many of the true predictions of our theory—from passed theorem-tasks to passed axiom-tasks—can be accounted for by the fact that the probability of our subjects passing LA1 was .50, the probability of passing LA2 was .73, and so on through all the solvable tasks? In fact, the analysis credits the rival theory with 136 correct predictions and 95 false ones out of 231 attempts. Our model is more useful than the current rival, in this situation, only if ours is correct more than 136 out of 231 times. As reported, our model actually predicts correctly in this situation 182 times and incorrectly 49 times. This result is 20% better than what would be expected on the basis of the current rival theory alone.

The logic of the analysis applies in the same way to the other kinds of predictions the theory makes (theorems to theorems, etc.). Overall, our model is 20% more accurate than the second hypothetical rival. When the predictions are broken down, this 20% margin is approximately preserved for all four types of predictions shown in Table 4, including the troublesome ones 46–52.

The Third Rival Theory

A third rival theory may be imagined which predicts the number of theorem-tasks and the number of axiom-tasks passed by each subject. Thus, this rival predicts that subject 1 will pass four axiom-tasks and two theorem-tasks, that subject 2 will pass four axiom-tasks and three theorem-tasks, and so on.

Now consider the passing-predictions of our theory proceeding from passed single theorem-tasks to other theorem-tasks, i.e., predictions 30–45 in Table 4. For each subject some number of predictions of this kind were made. For example, there were five such predictions for subject 3. Since subject 3 passed four out of eight, or .50 of his theorem-tasks, the expected number of correct predictions according to the rival theory is 5 × .50 or 2.50, and the number of false predictions is 2.50 also. If this same procedure is carried out on all 30 subjects, the rival theory leads us to expect that 101.8 of the 140 predictions of the real model would be confirmed and 38.2 of the predictions disconfirmed. If more of the predictions are confirmed than this, then the success of the real theory cannot be entirely accounted for by this third rival theory, if such existed. This third rival theory thus answers the question: How many true predictions of our theory—from passed, single, theorem-tasks to other passed theorem-tasks—can we explain by the fact that the probability of subject 1 passing a theorem-task is .25, the probability of subject 2 passing a theorem-task is .38, and so on for all 30 subjects? As reported earlier, our model makes 115 true predictions and 25 false ones in this situation. This result is 9% better than that expected under the rival theory alone.

The logic of the analysis applies in the same way to the other kinds of predictions the theory makes. For predictions A–C of

Table 4, the margin of superiority for the model is 17%, 6%, and 9%, respectively. But for the predictions D (46–52), the model is 32% *worse* than the rival. Adding in this poor performance, the real model exceeds the hypothetical rival by only 5% overall.

The Fourth Rival Theory

Suppose a theory existed which could predict both the probability over all subjects of passing each particular task, and also the probability over all tasks of each particular subject passing a task. This imagined theory could predict how many subjects passed each particular task, and also how many (solvable) tasks each subject passed. How much of the success of the real model follows equally well from this latest imagined rival theory?

In order to answer this question, imaginary data for 30 subjects were generated by means of random tables. The randomness of the draw was restricted by two conditions. The same number of imaginary subjects had to pass each task as in the real data, and each imaginary subject had to pass the same number of tasks as a matched real subject. Thus, between the real and random data, the same number of subjects passed each task, and the distribution across subjects of the number of tasks passed was the same. Then the identical analysis as carried out on the real data was performed on the random data. If the current rival theory can account for the real data, then the imaginary data should yield as great a proportion of true predictions as the real data.

The results of this analysis show that our model has here met its match. The theory predicts the real data only 4% more accurately than the random data. This result is not too disappointing if it is recognized how powerful a rival theory has been imagined. The fact that almost all of the success of our theory can be explained by the imagined theory does little to detract from our model, especially since this rival theory has not actually been discovered.

The Fifth Rival Theory: Commonsense Predictions

The last rival theory that will be examined is of a different nature than the four previous ones, since it is not imaginary. Instead of the elaborate logical apparatus constructed for our model, it may be asked whether there is a simpler theory that specifies the pattern of children's success on tasks as well as does our theory.

The fifth rival is such a theory. It predicts that tasks that employ the same operations are either all passed or all failed by each individual child. By "operations" are meant the manipulations of the sticks performed by the experimenter while the child is watching (see the description of the length tasks in Ch. 3, section 5). The predictions of this naive theory appear in Table 6. The tasks in part (a) of the table are paired because neither involves any operations. The tasks in (b) all involve the addition operation. The two tasks in (c) both involve the stacking operation. The tasks in (d) all involve the subtraction or the undoing operation. The tasks in (e) both involve the same operations as in (d) but further involve addition as well. Some predictions of this latest rival theory are predictions our theory makes also.

The data from the length experiment were analyzed in terms of these predictions. Every time a child passed or failed both of the tasks linked by a prediction, the commonsense theory was

TABLE 6

PREDICTIONS OF THE SIMPLE RIVAL THEORY FOR LENGTH TASKS

a. (i) LA1 ↔ LT1	c. (i) LA4 ↔ LT3
b. (i) LA3 ↔ LT2	d. (i) LA5 ↔ LT5
(ii) LA2 ↔ LT2	(ii) LA5 ↔ LT6
(iii) LA3 ↔ LT7	(iii) LT5 ↔ LT6
(iv) LA3 ↔ LA2	e. (i) LA6 ↔ LT4
(v) LT7 ↔ LT2	
(vi) LA2 ↔ LT7	

credited with a true prediction. Whenever a child passed one of the tasks of a prediction and failed the other, the rival was accorded a failure.

The results of the analysis revealed that this simple theory predicted correctly 243 times and incorrectly 117 times, giving it 68% accuracy. Our theory predicts 9% more accurately than this fifth rival. Our theory therefore accounts for the patterning of success and failures better than this less complex rival.

8
EXTENSION OF THE
MODEL FOR LENGTH

1. COMPETENCE AND PERFORMANCE
ASPECTS OF THE MODEL

Generally, our model for length is about 80% correct in its predictions. In this chapter and the next we will try to account for the 20% of wrong predictions, especially the poor results associated with predictions 46–52 of Table 4 (i.e., predicting success on one theorem-task from success on two other theorem-tasks). To achieve this, a "competence-performance," or "competence-automaton," distinction will be invoked. We shall not simply explain away embarrassing failure by the model, however, but will extend the model so as to yield testable predictions.

The distinction between what an organism knows (his competence) and what he can or will do with that knowledge (his performance) is not new to psychologists (e.g., Tolman, 1932, p. 364), although linguists like Chomsky (1965, 1968) have gone furthest toward demonstrating the distinction's importance. Flavell and Wohlwill (1969) explicate the difference between competence and automaton (= performance) variables in the context of "formal" and "functional" aspects of theory construction.

> ... a psychological theory that accounts for complex behavior will
> have two principal components: a *competence* model, which is a formal,

logical representation of the structure of some domain (e.g., the abstract rules for generating grammatical strings in some language); an *automaton* model . . . which represents the psychological processes by which the information embodied in competence actually gets accessed and utilized in real situations. The competence model gives an abstract, purely logical representation of what the organism knows or could do in a timeless, ideal environment, whereas the automaton model has the job of describing a real device that could plausibly instance that knowledge or skill, and instance it within the constraints (memory limitations, rapid performance, etc.) under which human beings actually operate [p. 71].

After making such a distinction it becomes crucial to establish behavioral indices of competence in order to make tests of hypotheses based on the distinction. A behavioral definition of competence will be proposed shortly. First let us assume that the model of the last section is entirely correct in its specification of the axiom-tasks, the theorem-tasks, and their relations. When the theoretical developments of the present section are put to the test, both new and old parts of the model will therefore be tested simultaneously.[1] To facilitate exposition, instead of referring to different axiomatic-processes in competence we shall refer instead to the axiom-tasks alleged to result from only one such process; recall (Ch. 6, section 2) that certain tasks were designated as axiom-tasks because of the belief that they overlay only one axiomatic-process.

The competence-performance distinction may be explicated for our model by the following definitions.

Definition 1: We shall say that a child *has an axiom-task in competence* (more briefly, *has an axiom-task*) if and only if either (*a*) he passes that axiom-task, (*b*) he passes one or more theorem-tasks that require that axiom-task ("requires" according to our model), or (*c*) both (*a*) and (*b*).

Since axiom-tasks trivially require themselves, this definition can be restated as follows. A child *has* an axiom-task if and only if he passes some task that requires that axiom-task according to our model.

---

[1] In this way we are open to all the ambiguities that result from a falsified but complex theory. What part, if not all, of the theory needs revision? The price seems unavoidable if a theory of logical thinking in children is to be adequate for its complex subject-matter.

Definition 2: We shall say that a child *has a theorem-task* if and only if he has all the axiom-tasks sufficient for that theorem-task, according to our model.

Five comments are necessary. (i) The need to assume the accuracy of our model is evident. The definitions of having axiom-tasks and theorem-tasks are embedded within a theory of the child's axiomatic processes for a set of logical tasks. (ii) From these definitions it follows that if a subject passes a theorem-task, then he has that theorem-task. Since passing an axiom-task also implies having it (by definition) the definitions credit a child with having in competence at least every task he passes. It also follows that a child has any task, theorem-task or axiom-task, that would be predicted for him at least once from Table 4. It does not follow, conversely, from the definitions, that the prediction of the absence of a task from a single contrapositive of Table 4 means that the child does not have that task. (iii) The decision to define having an axiom by the child's passing it or by passing at least *one* theorem-task that requires it, instead of two or even more theorem-tasks that require it, is to some extent arbitrary. Had each subject been administered twice as many tasks, the criterion for having an axiom may have been stiffened to passing the axiom or passing *two* theorem-tasks requiring it. In this way, the axiomatic-processes underlying the axiom-task would have to be operable to some more than minimal degree before being counted in the child's competence. Such a move might motivate a complementary change in the original model. Multiple evidence would be necessary before predictions such as those in Table 4 are made. (iv) Examination of Table 3 shows that some axioms have more opportunity for being counted in competence than others. For example, a child has LA5 if he passes any task among LA5, LT5, LT6, LT8 — four tasks in all. On the other hand, a child has LA6 if he passes any task among LA6, LT5, LT6 — only three tasks in all. This asymmetry is due to the choice of theorem-tasks to test. It is perhaps also partly due to the relative importance (frequency of use) of the axiomatic-processes, since the selection of tasks was more or less haphazard from the point of view of frequency of axiom-occurrence. In any event, the asymmetry will not have much affect on the forthcoming theoretical developments. (v) Definitions 1 and 2 boil down to saying that a subject has any task t in competence if and only if he passed any task or set of tasks, including t itself, that predicts its presence according to our model.

2. THE RELATION BETWEEN PASSING A TASK AND HAVING A TASK: FLAVELL AND WOHLWILL'S MODEL.

The relation between having a task in competence and showing it in performance has been carefully analyzed by Flavell and Wohlwill (1969). Their approach is captured in Eq. (8.1).

$$(8.1) \quad Pr(\text{passing task } T) = Pr(\text{having task } T) \times A_T^{1-k_c}$$

For a given child c, the probability of passing task T is equal to the probability that child c has task T, times the term $A_T^{1-k_c}$ which reflects performance factors. To explicate this last term as well as the whole conception of the equation, Flavell and Wohlwill (1969) will be quoted extensively, with changes made in their symbolic notation whenever convenient for our own purposes.

> We may now specify three parameters that jointly determine a child's performance: ... the probability that the operation will be functional in a given child; A, a coefficient applying to a given task or problem, and determining whether, given a functional operation, the information will be correctly coded and processed; and k, a parameter expressing the weight to be attached to the A factor in a given child. ...
>
> [The probability of having the task] reflects the degree to which a given operation has become fully established in a particular child. The assumption here is that ... these structures have a probabilistic character, appearing now in evidence, now absent. ... This uncertainty and instability ... may be expressed in terms of [the probability of having a task] changing from 0 in the preoperational period to 1.0 when the operation has become established.
>
> A, according to our model, is an attribute of the task. It represents the likelihood for any given task that the operation, if functional, will in fact be called into play, and its end product be translated into the desired output. The value of this factor may also be expected to vary between 0 and 1, depending on a host of factors related to task-difficulty; the stimulus

materials and their familiarity, the manner of presentation of the relevant information and the amount of irrelevant information from which it has to be abstracted, the sheer magnitude of the information load placed on the child in dealing with the problem, the role played by memory and sequential processing of information, and so on. . . .

Yet the influence of these task-related variables itself varies with age. For the average five-year-old the likelihood of success in placing a set of 10 stimuli in order of size may be considerably smaller than it would be for only 6 stimuli, for instance, whereas for a ten-year-old there may be little difference. This is the reason for introducing the parameter k, or more particularly its complement, $1-k$, as a power to which A is to be raised. The parameter is intended to express the weight that the A corresponding to a particular task carries for a given child, depending on that child's ability to abstract the information required to utilize a particular operation, and to code and process information generally. For the sake of simplicity, we shall assume that k varies from 0, at a relatively early phase of the establishment of an operation, to an ideal of 1.0, when the stage has become fully consolidated; accordingly, the influence of A, when raised to $(1-k)$, should be expected to decrease progressively over this period [Pp. 98–100].

We shall call the term A^{1-k} for a particular task and developmental level the *performance-factor* of that task for that developmental level. The term A_T alone (without exponent) is called the *automaton-term* for the task T. Note that according to Flavell and Wohlwill's conception, each task T has associated with it its own automaton term, A_T, and each child c has associated with him a parameter, k, reflecting his developmental level.

3. THE COMPETENCE-AUTOMATON MODEL APPLIED TO THE LENGTH-EXPERIMENT DATA

For the 30 subjects in the length experiment the probability of passing a particular task is estimated by the number of children who pass it divided by the 30 children who took it. The probability of having a task is estimated by the number of children who have it, divided by the 30 who took it. The tasks which each subject has is determined by Table 3 in conjunction with what he passed. For example, one of the subjects of the length experiment passed LA2, LA3, and LT4. Thus, he has LA2 and LA3 because he passed them. In addition he has LA1 and

LA4 by virtue of passing LT4 (see Table 3). Since he has these axioms, then by definition he has theorem-tasks LT1, LT2, LT3, LT4, and LT7. The tasks in competence for each subject were specified in this manner. The probability of having each task could then be calculated. The results are shown in Table 7.

With both the probability of passing and the probability of having each task, the A^{1-k} term, or performance-factor, may be determined for each task. This is achieved by dividing both sides of Eq. (8.1) by the probability of having the task in question. The result is equation (8.2), for any task T, and given developmental level, c.

(8.2) $\dfrac{Pr \text{ (passing task } T)}{Pr \text{ (having task } T)} = A_T^{1-k_c}$

TABLE 7

PROBABILITY THAT EACH LENGTH TASK IS IN COMPETENCE

Task	Probability
LA1	.90
LA2	.80
LA3	.93
LA4	.83
LA5	.50
LA6	.70
LT1	.90
LT2	.93
LT3	.83
LT4	.70
LT5	.47
LT6	.43
LT7	.83
LT8	.47

Since passing a task implies having it, Eq. (8.2) may be written equivalently as (8.3).

(8.3)
$$\frac{\text{Pr (pass task T and have task T)}}{\text{Pr (have task T)}} = \frac{\text{Pr (pass task } T\text{: have task } T)}{} = A_T^{1-k}$$

That is, the performance-factor is equal to the conditional probability of passing task T, given that task T is in competence. From (8.2) and (8.3) it follows that the greater the difficulty of overcoming the performance variables of a task, the lower the value of the performance-factor.

TABLE 8

PERFORMANCE-FACTORS FOR LENGTH TASKS

Task	Fraction	Decimal
LA1	15/27	.56
LA2	22/24	.92
LA3	23/28	.82
LA4	20/25	.80
LA5	6/15	.40
LA6	17/21	.81
LT1	22/27	.81
LT2	24/28	.86
LT3	21/25	.84
LT4	10/21	.48
LT5	12/14	.86
LT6	4/13	.31
LT7	11/25	.44
LT8	10/14	.71

Each of the 14 tasks yields its own performance-factor, at a given level of development, because the automaton term A varies with the task. For the moment, let us consider all 30 subjects to be in the same broad developmental level k and calculate the performance factors for each task. This number may be estimated by the number of children who pass the task divided by the number of children who have it (by Eq. (8.2)). The resulting performance-factors for each task appear in Table 8.[2]

Table 8 reveals that task LT6 has the lowest performance-factor. It therefore has the greatest amount of performance difficulties associated with it. LT7 also has a low performance factor. Recall the set of predictions that were most often disconfirmed. These were predictions 46–52 of Table 4, most of which predicted the presence of these same tasks, LT6 and LT7. Moreover, especially in the case of LT7, the predictions are made from tasks with considerably higher performance-factors. It seems understandable then, that predictions 46–52 should fail, even if the model's description of children's competence is accurate.

Have we just explained why our model fell down for predictions 46–52 of Table 4? Certainly not; through a devious route, the performance-factors of LT6 and LT7 are constrained to be low precisely because the theory falsely predicts their presence many times. By the same token, however, if the low value of these task's performance-factor could be independently explained, then we will have gone some way towards explaining and hence rationalizing the poor performance of our model for predictions 46–52. All the model's false predictions could be similarly ex-

---

[2] A few people who have seen Table 8 are dismayed by the fact that the performance-factors of the axiom-tasks are not impressively higher than those of the theorem-tasks, or at least the theorem-tasks relying on more than one axiomatic-process. It is felt that since the axiom-tasks overlay only one axiomatic-process, they should have less performance difficulties associated with them than theorem-tasks that require the joint action of two or more axiomatic processes. But such a belief does not follow from the notion of an axiom-task used here. It is just as plausible that axiomatic-processes increase the probability of the desired result when they interact. The issue is empirical.

plained. Accordingly, we must seek empirical support for Flavell and Wohlwill's model embodied in Eq. (8.1), since it defines performance-factors for tasks. In order to test the adequacy of our revised model, some predictions will be derived from it and tested against the data of the length experiment.

Let us summarize to this point. Our naive model of Chapter 6 performed well but also made some serious errors. To explain the model's shortcomings we have introduced a competence-automaton distinction as formulated by Flavell and Wohlwill (1969). The point of introducing the distinction is to save the original model on the level of competence, attributing its errors entirely to performance factors. The distinction has been operationalized by definitions that tie it closely to the former naive model. The job facing us now is to derive empirical predictions from the competence-performance assumptions and test them against the data from Experiment 3. In this way we hope to justify Eq. (8.1) and Definitions 1 and 2 so that we may ultimately use them to help explain the incorrect predictions our model has made.

4. A PREDICTION DERIVED FROM THE COMPETENCE-AUTOMATON EQUATION: DEVELOPMENTAL CHANGE OF k

One prediction of Eq. (8.1) may be developed as follows. According to the model the value of k increases with development from 0 to 1.0. Hence Eq. (8.2) shows that as development proceeds, the ratio of passing a particular task to having that task should increase also. This prediction is not as obvious as it might seem at first. As a child develops we expect him to pass more tasks, but this fact alone will increase the value of both the numerator *and* denominator of the left side of (8.2). The increase in k implies that the numerator of the fraction will increase faster than the denominator. In essence, the model's claim is that as development progresses, children show in performance more and more of their competence.

How can this prediction be tested? Evidently an index of development, that is, an index for k, must first be found. A dilemma immediately arises. The only available evidence of a subject's development is his performance on the length tasks. But if we divide children into two developmental groups on the basis of number of tasks passed, then our predictions about the effects of the k parameter are confounded: Due only to the increasing probability of passing a task, the ratio which measures the performance-factor will increase to an undetermined extent with development. At the limit, for children who pass every task, the ratio must equal 1.0. By choosing as an index of development the probability of passing tasks, we will have compelled the ratio to increase, to some unknown extent, by the mathematics of the situation alone.[3]

The dilemma was resolved by a simulation procedure. The analysis went as follows. The children were ordered by number of (solvable) tasks passed; the arrangement of children passing the same number of tasks was random. Two groups were formed, the first 15 children in one group, the second 15 in the other. Overall, children in the first group passed 63 tasks, whereas children in the second group passed 154 tasks. Table 9 presents the performance-factors for each group for each task. The table shows that for 12 of the 14 tasks, the ratio of passing a task to having the task does increase from group I to II, as predicted. By a binomial test this result is significant at the .006 level. But this binomial test assumes that the *a priori* probability of a difference in the predicted direction is .5. This assumption has just been questioned: The effects of the very definition of

---

[3]Prior to the length experiment each subject was administered a battery of Piagetian tests based mainly on the "conservation" notions. Could these be used as a measure of the development? Their use would occasion a new dilemma. To the extent that the Piagetian tests correlate with the number of length-tasks passed, the same confounding problem arises as before. To the extent that the Piagetian tests to do not correlate with the number of length-tasks passed, we have reason to suspect their validity as a measure of development with respect to length notions.

development on the differences between the groups must be sub-tracted out of the results of Table 9 in order to have a fair test of the empirical prediction derived from Eq. (8.2).

To achieve this unconfounding, new data were simulated and an analysis of them was compared to the results obtained with the real data. There were two methods of simulation. The first method was a randomization procedure. New data were generated by means of random tables with only the restriction that each task be passed by the same number of subjects as was true in the real data. For example, since 15 children passed LA1,

TABLE 9

PERFORMANCE-FACTORS FOR LENGTH-TASKS:
TWO DEVELOPMENTAL LEVELS

Task	Group I		Group II	
	Fraction	Decimal	Fraction	Decimal
LA1	2/12	.17	13/15	.87
LA2	8/10	.80	14/14	1.00
LA3	9/13	.69	14/15	.93
LA4	6/11	.55	14/14	1.00
LA5	0/3	.00	6/12	.50
LA6	6/7	.86	11/14	.79
LT1	8/12	.67	14/15	.93
LT2	9/13	.69	15/15	1.00
LT3	7/11	.64	14/14	1.00
LT4	2/8	.25	8/13	.62
LT5	2/3	.67	10/11	.91
LT6	1/2	.50	3/11	.27
LT7	2/10	.20	9/15	.60
LT8	1/2	.50	9/12	.75

15 passes were randomly distributed among the 30 imaginary subjects (with the others failing LA1). Then the same procedure was carried out with the imaginary subjects as was carried out with the real subjects. They were ordered according to the number of tasks passed and divided into two groups of 15 subjects each. As before, the probability of passing each task and the probability of having each task was estimated for each group by the proportion of children passing and having each task, so that the ratio A^{1-k} could be determined for each task for each group.

If the differences between groups I and II in Table 9 are due to something more than the way the developmental groups were defined, then for each task the differences in performance-factors between the randomly generated groups should not be as great as the same differences in Table 9. Comparison leaves the issue in some doubt. The real data show greater differences between the performance-factors of groups I and II than for the random data in only 10 of 14 cases. The same is true if one uses the ratios of the performance-factors associated with each developmental group. With a binomial test, this result is significant at the .09 level.

A second random draw was performed exactly like the one just described, and the same analysis carried out. This time 11 out of 14 of the differences between groups I and II of the real data were larger than the comparable differences in the simulated data. Such a result is significant beyond the .03 level. However, again only 10 out of 14 of the ratios of group I performance-factors to group II performance-factors were smaller for the real data than for the simulated data.

We tested how much of the difference between groups was attributable not just to the fact that children in group II passed more tasks overall than those in group I, but to the fact that group II passed exactly 154 tasks while group I passed exactly 63 tasks. New data were randomly generated as before, but with this additional restriction. Then we again counted how many children in each group passed each task and had each task, resulting in another set of pairs of performance-factors to compare to Table 9. Once again the results were ambiguous. If ratios of performance-factors were used, the real data ratios exceeded the generated data only 9 out of 14 times ($p < .2$ by binomial test). If differences between performance-factors of the groups were used, the real data exceeded the generated data as predicted 10 out of 14 times ($p < .09$).

Finally, random data were generated which respected the number of tasks passed by each child. That is, each imaginary subject was matched by a real subject who passed the same number of tasks. When the appropriate differences were studied, the real data exceeded the random data 11 out of 14 times ($p < .03$). When the ratios were used, this figure dropped to 9 of 14 times, an unreliable result. LA6 and LT6 were frequently among the tasks which gave greater results for the random data than for the real data.

The second method of simulating data was to calculate performance-factors from the marginal totals of each task and developmental level. Since group I passed 63 tasks out of 210 administered to them ($= 14$ tasks $\times$ 15 subjects), the probability of a task being passed in this group equals .30. Similarly, the probability of a task being passed by group II is $154/210 = .73$. We know also the overall probability of each particular task being passed. As shown in Table 1, the probability of passing LA1 $= .50$, and so on. Multiplying these two marginal distributions together (as in calculating expected values for a 14 $\times$ 2 contingency table) gives one estimate of the probability of a child from each group passing each task. It should be clear that these estimates are derived by assuming independence between the two marginal distributions. Hence we have another "rival model." This rival has perfect information about the difficulty of each task and the developmental level of each group. But it is wholly ignorant of the patterning of passes and failures for individual subjects. The latter, of course, is the concern of the model being elaborated in this volume.

To calculate performance-factors we need both the probability of passing tasks and also the probability of having tasks. An estimate of the probability of having each task for each group was calculated exactly the same way. This time the marginal distribution based on having tasks was employed. The quotients of the estimates of passing and having tasks gives a new set of performance-factors based on the assumption of independence.

The differences between the performance-factors of the two developmental groups for this latest simulated data are smaller than for the real data 10 out of 14 times ($p < .09$). Again the result is ambiguous.[4]

The results of the first attempt to derive testable consequences from the competence-performance extension of our model are thus equivocal.

5. THE DETERMINANTS PREDICTION

Another prediction from the model of Eq. (8.1) focusses on the exponential form of the performance-factor A^{1-k}. If the model is appropriate for characterizing the developmental changes in performance variables, and if the model of Chapters 6 and 7 has correctly identified the axiomatic-processes for our length-tasks, then an important deduction follows.

Consider any two developmental levels, conceptualized in our model as 1-k_I and 1-k_{II}, and consider the automaton terms associated with any two tasks, conceptualized as A_1 and A_2. Each combination of developmental level and automaton term will give a value between zero and one. By Eq. (8.2) this number is equal to the ratio of passing the task to having the task, for the given task and developmental level. According to the theory, each of these four numbers should be equal to one of $A_1^{1-k_I}$, $A_2^{1-k_{II}}$, $A_1^{1-k_{II}}$, $A_2^{1-k_I}$. Thus, these four entries of a table such as Table 9 could be represented theoretically as in Fig. 22. If the

---

[4]We did not compare the ratios of performance-factors for the groups because this number is a constant across tasks (it is .66) due to the method of calculation of the simulated performance-factors.

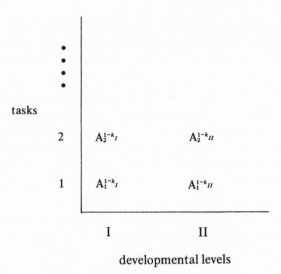

Fig. 22. Performance-factors for two tasks for each of
two developmental levels.

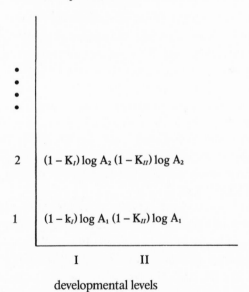

Fig. 23. Logarithms of performance-factors for two
tasks for each of two developmental levels.

logarithms of these performance-factors are taken, then theoretically these numbers should represent the entries in Fig. 23. The determinant of the 2 × 2 matrix represented in Fig. 23 equals $(1-k_I$ log $A_2)$ $(1-k_{II}$ log $A_1)$ − $(1-k_{II}$ log $A_2)$ $(1-k_I$ log $A_1)$. A simple rearrangement of terms shows that this determinant equals 0. In sum, the model makes the following prediction. Transform the table of performance-factors for the two developmental levels into a new table by taking the logarithms of the entries. Then the determinant of any 2 × 2 submatrix in the new matrix should equal zero.

To test this prediction against the data of the length experiment, the logarithms of the entries in Table 9 were calculated. The only exception is the logarithm of the performance-factor for developmental level I, task LA5. The logarithm in this case should be minus infinity. Because the performance-factor is based only on three observations, we have assigned it the more reasonable value of .1 instead of 0. This is less than any other performance-factor in the table. The logarithm of this more manageable value is −1.0.

When these logarithms are arranged according to task and developmental level (as in Table 9), 91 2 × 2 determinants result. Fifty-one of the determinants deviate from zero by .02 or less; 63 deviate by .04 or less; 72 of the determinants deviate by .06 or less; 19 of them deviate from zero by more than .06. To get an idea of how accurate these results are, the same analysis was performed on the simulated data described in the last subsection. The real results are comparatively accurate to the extent that the determinants for the simulated data deviate more widely from the predicted zero.

Recall that two of these random draws were restricted only by the popularity of tasks; the same number of imaginary subjects passed each task as did real subjects. For one of these two sets of data the number of determinants deviating from zero by no more than .02, .04, and .06 are 33, 47, and 59, respectively. For the other set, the number of determinants differing by .02, .04, and .06 are 33, 56, and 65. In both cases the real data conform considerably more accurately to the prediction than the random data. A similar analysis was performed for another set of random data described earlier. In this case, the same restriction on popularity of tasks was imposed as before, but there was an additional restriction as well: Fifteen of the imaginary subjects had to account for 63 of the passed tasks, and the other fifteen for 154 of the passed tasks. For these random data 41, 56, and 61 of the determinants were less than .02, .04, and .06, respectively. Again, the real data is accurate in comparison. The other random draw described earlier respected the number of tasks passed by each subject. For this data, 33, 62, and 85 of the determinants were less than .02, .04, and .06, respectively. Again the real data appear more accurate. We also took the logarithms of the performance-factors of the two simulated developmental groups calculated from the marginal totals of the real groups' performance. For these data, 37, 57, and 78 determinants were less than .02, .04, and .06, respectively—not as accurate as the real data. Finally, to see whether the superiority of the real data in these comparisons with simulated data hinges only on the order of magnitude of the logarithms and not on their arrangement in the table, the logarithms for the real data were randomly rearranged and the determinats taken again. The real data is again shown to conform to the determinants prediction comparatively well: For this last set of simulated data, 23, 39, and 53 of the determinants were less than .02, .04, and .06, respectively.

6. THE "BEST-FIT" PREDICTION

The last analysis sought support for the axioms of our model in conjunction with the exponential form of the performance-factor A^{1-k}. A more elegant way to explore the same issues was suggested to the writer by Dr. Michael Levine. By using this method, the "best" values (in a least-squares sense) of log A_i and $1-k_j$ can be determined for all tasks i, and for all developmental levels j up to a similarity transformation. Specifically, α log A_i can be determined for all tasks, and β $(1-k_j)$ can be determined for all developmental levels, α and β being unknown real numbers such that $\alpha\beta = 1$. As a result of this analysis it is possible to reconstruct the 28 performance-factors of Table 9 for all tasks and both developmental levels as accurately, in a least-squares sense, as would result from any other set of numbers selected for the αA_i's and β $(1-k_j)$'s. The reconstruction is achieved by multiplying the derived α log A_i's with the derived β $(1-k_j)$'s to get $(\alpha$ log $A_i)$ $(\beta$ $(1-k_j)$ $) = \alpha\beta$ $(1-k_j)$ (log A_i) $= (1-k_j)$ (log A_i) $=$ the logarithm of the performance-factor for the ith task and jth developmental level. The antilogarithm then yields the desired performance-factor.

This best-fit analysis is interesting only because the precise reconstruction of the observed performance-factors is not guaranteed by the mathematics of the procedure. To the extent that the performance-factors are reconstructed accurately, the data are consistent with a model such as ours which specifies one A_i for a given task regardless of developmental level, and one $1-k_j$ for a given developmental level, regardless of task, as well as the exponential relation between the two. We have then, as an empirical prediction of the model represented in Eq. (8.1) that such a best-fit analysis will permit a reconstruction of the performance-factors of Table 9 exactly — except for small deviations due to experimental error.

We shall briefly outline the procedure for finding the best fitting α log A_i's and β $(1-k_j)$'s. But we shall omit the mathematical derivation of the procedure, the derivation due to Dr. Levine. Call the matrix of the logarithm of the performance-factors (such as Table 9), P. Calculate $P^T P = S$ where P^T is the transpose of P. Find the smallest λ such that $|S - \lambda I| = 0$, where I is the identity matrix of the same dimensions as S. Then $(S - \lambda I)$ $(1-k_j)$ $= 0$ where $(1-k_j)$ is the vector of developmental levels. Divide by a constant to insure $\Sigma(1-k_j)^2 = 1$, and determine the values of the $(1-k_j)$'s. Then for each i set log $A_i = p_{ij}$ $(1-k_j)$ where p_{ij} are the entries in the original matrix of logarithms of the performance-factors.

With this method, the performance-factors of Table 9 were reconstructed. The derived values are shown in Table 10. The values in Table 10 are reasonably close to those in Table 9. In order to help judge the merit of the achieved accuracy, we performed the entire analysis over again starting from the performance-factor matrices associated with simulated sets of data. These simulations were among those used in the last subsection to test the determinants prediction. We shall not pause to give the results of the simulation analyses in detail. Similar to the

TABLE 10

LEAST-SQUARES RECONSTRUCTION OF PERFORMANCE-FACTORS
FOR THE TWO DEVELOPMENTAL LEVELS

Task	Group I	Group II
LA1	.19	.58
LA2	.81	.94
LA3	.71	.89
LA4	.58	.84
LA5	.10	.47
LA6	.81	.93
LT1	.68	.88
LT2	.72	.90
LT3	.67	.88
LT4	.25	.63
LT5	.67	.88
LT6	.36	.72
LT7	.20	.59
LT8	.49	.79

determinants prediction, the reconstruction of the simulated data was not as accurate as the reconstruction of the real data. To this extent the best-fit analysis corroborates the conclusion drawn from the determinants analysis: The Flavell-Wohlwill performance model of Eq. (8.1) is correct in portraying the performance-factors as a term referring to automaton variables unique to the task, weighted exponentially by a coefficient representing the developmental level of the subject.[5]

---

[5]Recall how closely wedded this competence-performance formulation is to the naive model of Chapters 6 and 7. Support for the former is also support for the choice of axioms of the latter.

9
AN ATTEMPT TO PREDICT THE PERFORMANCE-FACTORS

1. THE PURPOSE OF FURTHER THEORETICAL EXTENSION

To recapitulate, we have been concerned with finding empirical support for the competence-performance extension of our model. Predictions have been derived from Eq. (8.1) and tested against the experimental results. One prediction was that performance-factors increase with developmental level as measured by number of tasks passed. This prediction was verified, but perhaps only tentatively. Another prediction was that each 2×2 matrix of the logarithm of performance-factors in Table 9 would result in a determinant close to zero. Such a result would support the idea that performance-factors are representable by terms referring to automaton variables associated with tasks, weighted exponentially by a coefficient representing developmental level. The determinants prediction was well-confirmed. Finally, the same information gained from the determinants prediction was extracted a different way by a procedure that "fit" the observed performance-factors with numbers equal to the $\alpha \log A_i$'s and β $(1\text{-}k_j)$'s such that $\alpha\beta = 1$.

All the predictions tested so far are consequences of the model based on Grize's system in conjunction with the Flavell and Wohlwill model relating competence and performance. Nothing developed yet is able to specify the performance-factor $A^{1\text{-}k}$ for any task. To do this we shall require some new apparatus. We shall attempt to predict A^{1-k} for the theorem-tasks. We shall treat the subjects as one large developmental level. Rather than try to predict the axiom-tasks' performance-factors, we shall use information based on them in order to predict A^{1-k} for the theorem-tasks. Consequently, since the exact numbers which represent axiom-tasks' performance-factors are likely to change for different sets of theorem-tasks as well as for different sets of children, our method actually attempts to predict the relation between the performance-factors of axiom-tasks and theorem-tasks.

The importance of being able to predict the performance-factors of theorem-tasks is evident. We would then have taken a step toward explaining the poor performance of our naive model on predictions 46–52 of Table 4. These predictions said that success with certain theorem-tasks with high performance-factors implies success with other theorem-tasks which have considerably lower performance-factors. If the performance-factors of these theorem-tasks could be derived, we would have a basis for assigning probabilities to the assertions of the naive model, and perhaps come closer to an exact fit of the data.

The predictions and data analyses of the last chapter underlie the present attempt to predict performance-factors. In fact, the analysis of this subsection will be seen to presuppose the truth of the Flavell-Wohlwill model of competence and performance, and especially our axiom-bound definition of having a task. For this reason it was necessary to present evidence supporting that model before attempting to predict A^{1-k} for any task.

2. THE RELATIONSHIP BETWEEN PERFORMANCE-FACTORS OF THEOREM-TASKS AND PERFORMANCE-FACTORS OF COMBINATIONS OF RELEVANT AXIOM-TASKS

Consider the performance factor for the *pair* of tasks LA1 and LA3, that is, $A^{1-k}_{LA1\ \&\ LA3}$. This number is equal to the number of children who passed both tasks LA1 and LA3, divided by the number of children who have both LA1 and LA3. Now consider the performance-factor for LT7. The axioms for theorem 7 are axioms 1 and 3 (cf., Table 3). Hence, by the definition of having a task, the performance-factor for LT7, A_{LT7}^{1-k}, is equal to the number of children who pass LT7 divided by the number of children who have both LA1 and LA3. In short:

$$(9.1) \quad A_{LA1 \& LA3}^{1-k} = \frac{Pr \text{ (passing LA1 and LA3)}}{Pr \text{ (having LA1 and LA3)}}$$

$$A_{LT7}^{1-k} = \frac{Pr \text{ (passing LT7)}}{Pr \text{ (having LA1 and LA3)}}$$

Eqs. (9.1) show that the denominators of the two ratios measuring $A_{LA1 \& LA3}^{1-k}$ and A_{LT7}^{1-k} are equal. Therefore, to predict the performance-factor for LT7 from the performance-factor for LA1 and LA3, the relationship between the numerators must be determined. This analysis converts the problem of predicting one ratio from another into the simpler problem of predicting how much easier or more difficult it is to pass task LT7 than to pass both tasks LA1 and LA3. Similar considerations apply to any theorem-task. Given A^{1-k} for the combinations of axiom-tasks relevant to a theorem-task (by Table 3), we can predict the performance-factor of the theorem-task if we can predict the relative difficulty of passing that theorem-task compared to passing all the relevant axiom-tasks. It should be clear that per-formance-factors can be isolated in this way because of our judicious selection of axioms to pair with each theorem. The competence required for passing a given theorem-task is the same as that required for passing its relevant axiom-tasks. Relevancy is determined here again by appeal to the original form-alism. Competence being equated, the residual difference be-tween the difficulty of passing a given theorem-task and the dif-ficulty of passing all its relevant axiom-tasks may be ascribed to performance variables. Table 11 gives the performance-factors

TABLE 11

PERFORMANCE-FACTORS OF THEOREM-TASKS AND
PERFORMANCE-FACTORS OF THE RELEVANT
COMBINATIONS OF AXIOM-TASKS

Theorem-task		Relevant axiom-tasks	
LT1	.81	LA1	.56
LT2	.86	LA3	.82
LT3	.84	LA4	.80
LT4	.48	LA1– LA4	.57
LT5	.86	LA1, LA5, LA6	.21
LT6	.31	LA1, LA3, LA5, LA6	.23
LT7	.44	LA1, LA3	.56
LT8	.71	LA1–LA5	.36

for theorem-tasks and for their constellations of relevant axiom-tasks.

If the axiom-tasks conformed to a perfect Guttman-like scale, then to compare a given theorem-task to more than one axiom-task, the theorem-task would be compared to only the most difficult of the axiom-tasks. Because of the Guttman scale the other axiom-tasks would be passed if that one were passed. But since scalability in this sense is foreign to the theory elaborated here, a means of comparing ease of tasks is sought which does not presuppose scalability. The method adopted involves characterizing all the tasks along the same set of dimensions, different tasks meriting different values along some or all of the dimensions. The dimensions are then weighted as to their importance for the difficulty of tasks.

3. DIMENSIONS AND WEIGHTS

The tasks can be characterized by an indefinite number of dimensions. The problem is to choose those bearing on the difficulty of tasks. Theoretical motivation for the selection of the dimensions can be obtained by going back to the coordination rule that converts the formulas of Grize's axiomatization into tasks for the child (Chapter 5). If the coordination rule has done its job, then the task-features it specifies should be just those that determine its relative ease or difficulty, given the underlying competence. To see the point, reconsider the competence-performance distinction drawn by Flavell and Wohlwill (1969). Competence for them is captured in the abstract formalism of a theory. Grize's axiomatization fulfills this role in our model. Performance variables arise in the course of a real problem that exemplifies the formalism. It is the coordination rule that induces the actual tasks in which performance variables play a role. The formal and semantic sides of the theory thus correspond respectively to competence and performance variables in the child. In our present attempt to predict performance factors, it seems natural to use as relevant dimensions of tasks those dimensions given by the coordination rule.

Returning to the discussion of Chapter 5, we said that the bulk of the rule was achieved by interpreting the quadruple $<M, \leqslant, +, ->$. M, the set of variables, x, y, z, etc., is interpreted as the different colors represented by the sticks. The first dimension of tasks, then, is the number of different colors represented by the sticks in a given task.[1] The relation $\leqslant$ is interpreted as a difference in size between two sticks. For our second dimension we shall count the number of distinct sizes represented by the sticks at the beginning of a task. For example, if all the sticks are the same length at the start of a task (e.g., LT1, LT3), then there is only one size represented. The operation $+$ is interpreted two ways by the coordination rule, as addition and as stacking (see Ch. 3, section 5 for these operations). The third and fourth dimensions are thus the number of times these operations occur in a task. The operation $-$ is interpreted as subtraction, and the

---

[1] We shall honor the mistake of LT4 (c.f., footnote 1, Chapter 5). It is thus attributed two colors rather than the three it should have.

number of times this occurred in a task counts as the next dimension. As a final dimension, we depart from the coordination rule, but in a natural way. This last dimension is the number of relevant axiom-tasks for the given theorem-task, minus one. This dimension is included because in comparing the performance-factors of the theorem- and relevant axiom-tasks, account must be taken of the relative difficulty of passing two or more tasks as compared to only one task.

These dimensions are chosen because they were spelled out by the coordination rule. Other dimensions of tasks are affected by the rule but are not explicitly mentioned. Examples are the time it took to perform each task, the maximum number of sticks or stick-fragments on the stage at one time, the number of sentences spoken by E, and the operation of "undoing" (c.f., Ch. 3, section 5). Should these last dimensions prove to be the ones capable of predicting performance-factors, then a theoretically more interesting coordination rule than the present one would specify them.

The next question which arises is the relative importance of the dimensions specified, or as we shall say, the *weighting function* of each dimension. The weighting function carries the value of a task on a dimension into some number representing the performance difficulties associated with that aspect of the task. One fixed set of weighting functions for the dimensions is sought which will predict the performance-factors of all possible theorem-tasks, including LT1–LT8. To change the weights for every theorem-task would deprive our method of any significance.

Unfortunately, no theoretical considerations seem latent anywhere in the model to help us answer the question of weights. What is needed is a theory, e.g., of memory or information-processing, to predict how well children deal with the values of each task along each dimension. In lieu of such theoretical support, we must be content with the most empirical of courses. We simply search for those weighting functions that minimize the difference between the predicted and observed theorem-tasks—provided those weighting functions meet certain conditions specified directly below. Given such latitude with the weights, the predictions associated with the model's coordination rule is as follows: A set of (acceptable) weighting functions can be found which predict the performance-factors of theorem-tasks in conjunction with the dimensions specified by the coordination rule. We shall see, however, that the specific weighting functions need not be determined to decide whether the dimensions specified by the coordination rule are adequate for the present problem.

4. ADEQUACY OF THE DIMENSIONS FOR PREDICTING PERFORMANCE-FACTORS OF THEOREM-TASKS

The prediction of theorem-task performance-factors from the performance-factors of appropriate combinations of axiom-tasks proceeds as follows. All the tasks are given their proper value along each dimension. This is achieved in the task $\times$ dimension matrix of Table 12. For example, task LA3 involves sticks of three colors and three sizes; it has two addition operations, and no other kind of operations. With Table 12 completed, the value of each theorem-task on each dimension is subtracted from the largest value along that dimension of the axiom-tasks that are relevant (by Table 3) to that theorem. This step can be clarified by example. The difficulty of passing LT4 is to be compared to the difficulty of passing LA1, LA2, LA3, and LA4. On dimension (i), the number of differently colored sticks in the task, LT4 scores 2, and LA1–LA4 score 3, 2, 3, and 2, respectively. The difference between LT4 and LA1–LA4 on this dimension accordingly is max(3, 2, 3, 2) − 2 = 3 − 2 = 1, because 3 is the largest value of dimension (i) for the axiom-tasks relevant to LT4. The value 1 is entered in row LT4, column (i) of Table 13. All the cells in columns (i) – (v) of Table 13 are filled in similar fashion. The idea behind the procedure is that a child who has no difficulty with a particular value along some dimension of a task will have no difficulty with any lesser value along

TABLE 12

DIMENSION ANALYSIS OF THE LENGTH TASKS

	Dimensions				
Tasks	(i) No. of colors	(ii) No. of sizes	(iii) Add. ops.	(iv) Stack ops.	(v) Sub. ops.
LA1	3	3	0	0	0
LA2	2	2	2	0	0
LA3	3	3	2	0	0
LA4	2	2	0	1	0
LA5	3	3	0	0	1
LA6	2	2	1	0	1
LT1	3	1	0	0	0
LT2	3	2	2	0	0
LT3	1	1	0	1	0
LT4	2	1	1	0	0
LT5	3	3	0	0	2
LT6	3	3	0	0	2
LT7	4	4	1	0	0
LT8	2	1	0	0	1

that same dimension. For this reason only the largest value on each dimension for the relevant axiom-tasks are important. Table 13 also shows an additional column, labeled "surplus tasks." This sixth column gives the number of relevant axiom-tasks for each theorem, minus 1. (This dimension was discussed just above.)

Table 13 is designed to reflect the difference in complexity of each set of relevant axiom-tasks compared to each given theorem-task, as broken down by dimension. Positive numbers represent greater complexity for the sets of relevant axiom-tasks;

TABLE 13

DIMENSION ANALYSIS OF THE LENGTH TASKS: COMPARISON

	Dimension					
Task	(i) No. of colors	(ii) No. of sizes	(iii) Add. ops.	(iv) Stack ops.	(v) Sub. ops.	(vi) Surplus tasks
LT1	0	2	0	0	0	0
LT2	0	1	0	0	0	0
LT3	1	1	0	0	0	0
LT4	1	2	1	1	0	3
LT5	0	0	1	0	−1	2
LT6	0	0	2	0	−1	3
LT7	−1	−1	1	0	0	1
LT8	1	2	2	1	0	4

negative numbers represent less complexity. To derive a given theorem-task's performance-factor from that of the relevant set of axiom-tasks, it will thus be necessary to add to the latter if the numbers in the theorem-task's row are positive. This is because positive numbers indicate greater performance complexity for the set of relevant axiom-tasks. In turn, this means that the performance difficulties for the theorem-task are comparatively less, and this implies a comparatively *higher* performance-factor for the theorem-task. The reasoning is analogous if the numbers are negative.

The weighting function determines the relative importance of the numbers in the cells of Table 13. We make the empirical assumption that an increase on any of the dimensions, holding the others constant, can only make a task more difficult. This proposition seems plausible for the dimensions given by the coordination rule. The weighting function is thus required to be monotonically increasing. This condition is connected to the use of "max" of the values along each dimension of the relevant axiom-tasks. If a weighting function declined, then increasing values could make a task easier.

The weighting functions may now be used to predict theorem-task performance-factors. In general the procedure is as follows: Call the (monotonically increasing) weighting functions w_1, ..., w_6, and the values in Table 13 for a particular theorem-task i, c_{i1}, ..., c_{i6}. As described, c_{ij} represents the relative complexity of theorem-task i as compared to its relevant axiom-tasks, along dimension j. Then the total effect of all the dimensions is determined by some function f of the results for each dimension, as in Eq. (9.2).

$$(9.2) \; f[w_1(c_{i1}), \ldots, w_6(c_{i6}), A_{Relevant\ axioms}^{1-k}]$$

The number $A_{Relevant\ axioms}^{1-k}$ is the performance-factor for the constellation of axiom-tasks relevant to the theorem-task. It must be included in the function f since it is the baseline from which the performance-factor of the theorem-task is drawn. Why the performance-factor for the relevant constellation of axiom-tasks serves as the baseline for predicting the theorem-task performance-factors was explained in connection with Eq. (9.1) above. There is an important restriction on the function f in Eq. (9.2) which is similar to the increasing monotonicity requirement on the weighting functions, w. Whereas it is a logical possibility that tasks become overall less complex as they become more complex on each dimension, the more usual finding would almost certainly be the opposite. Hence, the function f must be such that $f(n_1, \ldots, n_k)$ is greater than $f(m_1, \ldots, m_k)$ if $n_1 > m_1$, ..., $n_k > m_k$. As an example of a function with this property, f might sum the $w_j(c_{ij})$'s across dimensions, and multiply the result by the performance-factor of the relevant axioms of the theorem in question.

But once these plausible assumptions about the functions w and f are made, study of Table 13 shows that no matter what weighting-functions, w, and function to combine weighting-functions, f, are constructed, serious mistakes will be made in the prediction of theorem-task performance-factors. For, the values in Table 13 in conjunction with the performance-factors of the relevant axiom-tasks in Table 11 are such that the performance-factor for LT4 must be greater than that for LT1 and LT5, the performance-factor for LT6 must be greater than that of LT5, and the performance-factor of LT8 must be greater than that of LT5. But all these statements contradict the real data on performance-factors given in Table 8.

Nor will it help to change some of the dimensions of the table while remaining within the coordination rule. For example, eliminating dimension (vi), surplus tasks for the axioms, will not help. Neither will adding a new dimension called "total number of operations," since the result would only be to give LT4 and LT8 the value of +1 for this dimension, and 0 to all other theorem-tasks, in·Table 13. We might hope to improve matters by giving importance to the equality relation between sticks. This could be achieved by having a dimension that is the number of sticks on the stage at the start of a task. But again this would simply worsen matters by assigning +2 to LT4 and LT8 and 0 to the other theorem-tasks in Table 13. It is true that we could add a dimension for the occurrence of zero-elements in a task, and thus cure one of the difficulties with an *ad hoc* weight for that dimension (since it would only apply to LT8), but the other serious difficulties would remain.

We are forced to conclude that the coordination rule for length does not specify all the features that are relevant to the role of automaton variables in children's performance on the length tasks. Whether the rule could be revised so as to better predict performance-factors of theorem-tasks, without changing the tasks so as to cause other facets of the model to fail, is an open question.

10
THE MODEL FOR CLASS-INCLUSION

1. THE PROBLEM OF DISCONFIRMATION

In Chapter 8 the competence-performance distinction was incorporated into the naive model of Chapter 6. The purpose of this theoretical extension was to help account for some serious false predictions on the part of the original model. The following question naturally arises: When should a model be salvaged in this way? How can we tell if the wrong model is being protected? When are we rationalizing the false predictions of a basically sound theory, and when are we simply on the wrong track? There seems to be no easy answer to these questions, although "simplicity" or "elegance" are sometimes invoked.

The question becomes poignant as the data of the class-inclusion experiment are examined. We shall conclude that the naive version of the model does so poorly that it is pointless to attempt to save it by appeal to Flavell and Wohlwill's competence-performance model. The reader is forewarned that no argument is offered which compels such a conclusion.

2. PERFORMANCE OF THE CLASS-INCLUSION MODEL

The class-inclusion data were analyzed to test the model in the same way as described for the length data, with two exceptions. First, it will be recalled that different children in the class-inclusion experiment were administered different theorem-

TABLE 14
PASSING PREDICTIONS FOR THE MODEL
FOR CLASS INCLUSION

A. Axioms to Theorems
 1. CA3 → CT1
 2. CA1 & CA3 & CA4 → CT4
 3. CA1 & CA5 & CA6 → CT5
 4. CA1 & CA3 & CA5 & CA6 → CT6
 5. CA1 & CA3 → CT7
 6. CA1 & CA3 & CA4 & CA5 → CT8

B. Theorems to Axioms
 7. CT1 → CA1
 8. CT2 → CA3
 9. CT3 → CA4
10. CT4 → CA1
11. CT4 → CA3
12. CT4 → CA4
13. CT5 → CA1
14. CT5 → CA5
15. CT5 → CA6
16. CT6 → CA1
17. CT6 → CA3
18. CT6 → CA5
19. CT6 → CA6
20. CT7 → CA1
21. CT7 → CA3
22. CT8 → CA1
23. CT8 → CA3
24. CT8 → CA4
25. CT8 → CA5

C. One Theorem to
   Another Theorem
26. CT7 → CT2
27. CT4 → CT2
28. CT4 → CT7
29. CT6 → CT5
30. CT6 → CT7
31. CT6 → CT2
32. CT8 → CT4
33. CT8 → CT7
34. CT8 → CT2

D. Two Theorems to
   a Single Theorem
35. CT4 & CT5 → CT6
36. CT5 & CT7 → CT6
37. CT5 & CT8 → CT6
38. CT2 & CT6 → CT7
39. CT4 & CT5 → CT8
40. CT4 & CT6 → CT8

tasks, and that no child was given the task resulting from axiom 2 (because of its trivial nature). Moreover, no child was administered a task CT1 or CT3 (see Ch. 5, section 3). Except for these details, the earlier discussion of the model for the length data may be consulted again for the mechanism and testing of the class-inclusion model. This mechanism generates the passing-predictions listed in Table 14. Predictions 35–40 of Table 14, the ones that gave such trouble to the length theory, were not testable for class-inclusion because of insufficient observations. This is the second exception. But judging from the pass-rates for formulas given in Table 2, we might expect that these latter predictions would be as troublesome for the class-inclusion as for the length model. The reason is that the difficult tasks CT6 and CT8 are predicted from relatively easier tasks, just as happened for length. Recall that these predictions substantially lowered the overall margin of superiority for the length model with respect to the third rival model.

Even without these potentially troublesome predictions the results for the class-inclusion model are not impressive. To help assess its merit, the class-inclusion model's performance will be compared to that of the length model. Later we shall speculate about reasons for the results of the comparison. The passing predictions of the class-inclusion model were correct 67% of the time (241 true predictions, 119 false predictions) compared to 76% for length. The failing predictions of the class-inclusion model were correct 62% of the time, compared to 81% for length. This difference between the performance of the class-inclusion and length models cannot be attributed to the proportion of children passing and failing tasks in the two experiments. The proportions were remarkably similar. The length subjects passed 51.7% of their (solvable) tasks, while the class-inclusion subjects passed 51.4% of theirs.

It would be nonetheless unwise to give too much credence to this superficial analysis of the relative merits of the length and class-inclusion models. The probability distributions for the proportion of true predictions, given various restrictions on the number of subjects passing different tasks, the number of tasks passed by different subjects, etc., is entirely unknown. As a consequence, we shall compare the class-inclusion model to the same hypothetical rival theories against which the length model was compared (Chapter 7).[1] By contrasting the relative performance of the two models against their rivals, we will have a basis for comparing the length and class-inclusion models. The rival models are a suitable yardstick for this purpose because their success depends entirely on the peculiarities of the data from which they are derived. Theoretically irrelevant differences in the marginal distributions of the data from the two experiments are therefore at least partially controlled for.

When the class-inclusion model makes predictions based on the relation of the axiom-tasks the child passed to the theorem-tasks he passed (predictions 1–6 in Table 14), it is correct 68% of the time (length: 81%). A hypothetical rival theory which could predict the overall probability of passing a theorem-task can be expected to be correct only 50% of the time. The real theory is thus 18% better than the rival theory (length: 34%). A rival theory which can predict the proportion of children passing each particular theorem-task would yield 60% true predictions. The real model for class-inclusion is only 8% better than this rival (length: 22%). The hypothetical rival theory which can predict how many theorem-tasks each child passed, can make 62% true predictions, giving the class-inclusion model only a 6% edge (length: 17%).

When predicting from theorems to axioms, and from single theorems to other single theorems (predictions 7–34 of Table 14) the pattern of results is the same: The class-inclusion model is better than the weakest of the three hypothetical rival theories of Chapter 7. But it is not consistently better than the other two. The corresponding margins of superiority for the length model are generally 15% or more greater than the margins for the class-inclusion model.

---

[1]The fourth hypothetical rival (Chapter 7) was not used because the required random simulation would be very difficult to achieve for the class-inclusion data. In the ensuing discussion, only the first three hypothetical rivals are considered, as well as the simple alternative (commonsense) theory of Chapter 7.

TABLE 15

	Exceeds in % true predictions	
	Class-inclusion	Length
Rival I	15	25
Rival II	7	20
Rival III	5	5

Table 15 summarizes the overall performance of the class-inclusion model with respect to the three hypothetical rivals of Chapter 7. It also gives the comparable figures for the length model.

A commonsense, uncomplicated rival theory can be constructed for the class-inclusion experiment, just as it was for the length experiment. As with length, the commonsense theory for class-inclusion predicts that tasks involving the same operations are passed or failed together. These predictions are listed in Table 16.[2] CA4 and CT8 are not mentioned since they are dissimilar to the other tasks, and to each other with respect to their operations. The real class-inclusion model exceeds the commonsense rival in accuracy by 9% for passing predictions. Here it is comparable to the length model which was superior to its commonsense rival also by 9% for passing-predictions.

If we use the rival theories as a metric with which to compare the performance of the length and class-inclusion models, the

[2]The commonsense theory for class-inclusion makes somewhat different predictions than its length counterpart. How can this be if the same formulas underlie both sets of tasks? The point is precisely that the commonsense theory takes no account of the formulas of the model but only of the tasks themselves.

TABLE 16

CLASS-INCLUSION COMMONSENSE THEORY

CA3 ↔ CT2
CA5 ↔ CT5
CA5 ↔ CT6
CA3 ↔ CT7
CT7 ↔ CT2
CT5 ↔ CT6
CT4 ↔ CA3
CT4 ↔ CT2
CT4 ↔ CT7

length model is shown to perform in a superior fashion. Its comparative success is more telling since the class-inclusion model was not saddled with the potentially troublesome predictions corresponding to 46–52 of Table 4. The superiority of the length model does not compel any particular evaluation of how well the class-inclusion model does independently of a comparison with length. But evidently the class-inclusion model is not impressive as an attempt to delineate children's axioms for class-inclusion principles. Accordingly, an attempt to explain the failings of the model by means of the competence-performance distinction of Chapter 8 does not seem warranted. The class-inclusion model does not provide reason to believe that the axiomatic-processes have been specified, and that the greater than 35% error of the model may be attributed to automaton variables alone.

3. EXPLANATION OF THE SUPERIORITY OF THE LENGTH MODEL

Why did the length model do better than the class-inclusion model? Aside from the possibility of relevant differences in the subjects for the two experiments, or poor experimental method, there are at least four possible reasons.

Difference in Theses for the Experiments

The first possibility is that the results were biased by the fact that only a subset of the axioms and theorems interpreted into tasks for the length experiment were interpreted into tasks for the class-inclusion experiment. Children in the latter study were not given a task CA2, CT1, or CT3, the axiom-task CA2 being taken out of consideration in the same way as other uninterpreted axioms. Thus, for the class-inclusion subjects, the model was not allowed to make a variety of predictions that were made by the length model for the length subjects. It is possible that the superiority of the length model would disappear had both models been tested on the same predictions. To control for this possibility, all the length data were reanalyzed for the length model, but this time tasks LA2, LT1, and LT3 were ignored. The predictions of the length model are now exactly those of the class-inclusion model as listed in Table 14. The predictions 46–52 of Table 4 were not analyzed since the comparable predictions 35–40 of Table 14 were not analyzed for class-inclusion. The number of these predictions is small for length, as it was for class-inclusion, since prediction 46 of Table 4 is lost (due to the omission of LT1). Similarly, the contrapositives of these predictions were not analyzed for the failing predictions.

The result of this reanalysis was that the length model generally performed as well as before. With respect to the "reduced" data, the model predicted passing correctly 76% of the time (280 true predictions, 43 false predictions). This result is the same as the model's performance on the full set of data. The situation is comparable when the reduced length-model is compared to the four rival models against which the class-inclusion and length models were tested. The percentage by which the real length-model outstripped the rival models remained about the same for the reduced data. More often there was an increase rather than a decrease in the new analysis. The situation is the same when the failing predictions are considered.

From these analyses we may conclude that the superiority of the length model is not due to the difference between the theses interpreted into tasks in the two experiments, especially since there is no guarantee that the class-inclusion model would have profited from the missing tasks.

Choice of Theorems

Had different theorems been interpreted into tasks, the results might have been entirely different. The last analysis does not rule out this possibility. The class-inclusion model might have performed impressively with different theorem-tasks, and the length model might have performed poorly. This is the second possible reason for the difference between the two models: Out of the large set of possible theorem-tasks, those haphazardly chosen were atypically unfortunate for the class-inclusion model, or atypically fortunate for the length model. There is no way to test this hypothesis solely on the basis of the current data.

Choice of Coordination Rules

The third possibility is that our coordination rules are not typical. Of all the rules that result in class-inclusion and length tasks, the ones selected might have fortuitously resulted in a superior length model. If some perhaps slight change in the coordination rules were made, the relative performance of the two models might be altered. Only new studies with different test materials can shed light on this possibility.

Differences in the Axiomatic Processes

The fourth possibility is the most interesting theoretically. *A priori*, it is possible that the axiomatic processes for class-inclusion and length abilities are functionally similar. The child might use the same logical principles for these two different domains. According to this theory, the child only changes the input-evaluators and the output, when he does length tasks as opposed to class-inclusion tasks. But the present data argue against such a possibility. The same abstract principles, embodied in Grize's formalism, yield models of different merit when they are translated into tasks dealing with length and class-inclusion. Hence, the child's competence for length relations seems to be structurally isomorphic to a formalism that is not structurally isomorphic to his class-inclusion competence. The two competences are therefore probably not structurally isomorphic to one another. Such a difference in the organization of length and class concepts would explain the superiority of the length model: Grize's formalism describes the structure of length concepts in the child, but not the structure of class concepts.

It is conceivable that another model could be devised that could account for both class-inclusion and length abilities, by some change in appropriate parameters. But given that the other possible explanations for our data are not entirely true, then the construction of such a model would not alter the point made here. Children are in some sense organized differently for class-inclusion than for length-relation concepts. The difference in the performance of our length and class-inclusion models resulted from the inescapable fact that as development proceeds length tasks arrive in the child's repetoire in a different pattern than do the logically analogous class-inclusion tasks. This finding is theory-free. It argues for the proposition that length and class-inclusion abilities partake of somewhat different cognitive processes. Nor is this conclusion suprising in light of the spatial, visualizable nature of length and the abstract, nonvisualizable nature of classes.[3]

The Piagetian position on this point would probably be that the axiomatic processes for the two domains are similar. This would be claimed because the two coordination rules induce tasks related to two of the Piagetian groupings, and all the groupings operate according to the same general laws (see Chapter 1). It was this generality that led Grize to construct one axiomatization for all eight groupings. Hence, our data con-

---

[3]The *members* of a class might well be visualizable, but the class made up of those objects is a much less tangible entity. Moreover, a class has far different properties than its members, e.g., the members of the class of apples can be eaten, but the class itself cannot.

tradict what seems to follow from Piagetian theory. It should be emphasized, however, that our results are in need of replication and extension before any firm conclusions may be drawn.

In the next chapter we examine the larger question of whether Piagetian theory should predict that our models for class-inclusion and length will be accurate. The narrower question of whether Genevans are contradicted by the differential predictive value of the two models is not raised again.

11
THE RELATION OF THE THEORY
TO GENEVAN PSYCHOLOGY

1. THE PURPOSE OF GRIZE'S FORMALISM

Piaget has founded a discipline he calls *genetic epistemology*, which will be described shortly. According to Piaget (1970a, pp. 15–16) the first rule in this discipline is collaboration among specialists from diverse fields. Jean-Blaise Grize is one such specialist who participated at the Center for Genetic Epistemology in Geneva. In Piaget's words (1963): "J. B. Grize is a pure logician, but one of the specialties that he shows at our Center is to grasp the interest of the specifics of psychogenetic analysis, and to invent . . . logical and algebraic models that correspond to the facts, not in their detail, but in their most important characteristics [p. 5]."

The formalism of Chapter 2 is an example of Grize's work. It is part of a larger attempt to provide an axiomatization of natural numbers "which follows a path closer to their real (psychological) genesis" than standard treatments of the logical foundations of number (Grize, 1960, p. 70). In the course of developing the axiomatization for number, he provides an axiomatization for Piaget's grouping model of concrete operational thought, since Grize is convinced by the Genevan position (Piaget, 1942, 1965) that numbers result from the fusion of groupings. It is this axiomatization of the grouping that was presented in Chapter 2. Piaget is quite enthusiastic about Grize's system and often alludes to it (e.g., Piaget, 1963, p. 5; 1967d, p. 83; Beth & Piaget, 1961, p. 186ff). What psychological significance does Piaget ascribe to Grize's axiomatization?

2. GENETIC EPISTEMOLOGY

The discipline of genetic epistemology is concerned with the traditional problems of epistemology but employs the tools both of empirical science and of formal logic. Logic has always played a role in epistemology. Piaget's innovation is to introduce the results of scientific investigation whenever a question of fact arises in an epistemological controversy, in place of unwarranted assertions of fact or entirely implicit assumptions of fact (Piaget, 1957c, 1970a). It follows that a premise of genetic epistemology is that epistemological questions actually do hinge on matters of fact much of the time. Piaget (1970b, pp. 7–8) is convinced that this premise is true.

Naturally, psychology is one of the most useful sciences for genetic epistemology. Developmental psychology is of special interest since Piaget believes that the structure of adult knowledge can only be understood in light of the origins of that knowledge in childhood (Piaget, 1950a, pp. 12–18; Piaget, 1967a, pp. 125–127; Piaget, 1970b, p. 1).

The reliance on empirical investigation does not make genetic epistemology into one more science, however. Piaget (1970b, p. 10) maintains that the purely formal, and thus empirically vacuous, procedures of mathematics and logic are equally important (see also Beth & Piaget, 1961, p. 274; Piaget, 1970a).

How do the empirical and formal sides of genetic epistemology interact to shed light on epistemological issues? The program may be summarized (Beth & Piaget, 1961) as follows:

> The axiomatician, to demonstrate the validity of a system, tries to reduce it to the weakest and least numerous set of axioms possible. . . . The psychologist, on the other hand, to explain the formation of an [intellectual] structure pursues a regressive analysis . . . and explanation is

achieved when he finds those elementary structures from which the new structure has been drawn, as well as the operations by means of which the passage was carried out. It may be seen, then, that between axiomatic reconstruction and genetic reconstruction there exists this global or functional analogy of a search for the most elementary conditions which account for a [formal] system or an [intellectual] structure. . . . But what we now assume is that there is at least a heuristic question which may be stated as follows. Let us call 'elementary axiomatic conditions' the axioms which are necessary and sufficient to formally deduce a system, and 'elementary genetic conditions' the beginning structures as well as the actions or operations which have permitted the passage from these structures to those whose formation require explanation. The question is then to establish in each particular case if there exists a relation between the axiomatic elements and the genetic elements such that understanding the former helps in analyzing the latter [p. 268].

As seen in this passage, and explicitly affirmed by Piaget elsewhere (1970b), "the fundamental hypothesis of genetic epistemology is that there is a parallelism between progress made in the logical and rational organization of knowledge and the corresponding formative psychological processes [p. 13]." By finding the parallelism, light is shed on both psychological and epistemological issues.

Lest Piaget's program appear to court Logicism (i.e., the confusion of empirical fact with logical validity), it should be pointed out that Piaget is well aware of the dangers of the fallacy (e.g., 1949, 1957b, p. 1).[1] In a similar vein, it should be stressed that Piaget does not claim that the logical structures he discovers to be isomorphic to some aspect of intellectual functioning have a conscious psychological representation. In fact, he explicitly denies this (Inhelder & Piaget, 1958, p. 321; 1964, pp. 281–282).

3. TWO TYPES OF LOGIC

It is crucial at this point to introduce a distinction Piaget (1957b) makes between two kinds of formalism: "as far as formalization is concerned, logic can be conceived from two distinct points of view: (1) logic as an *operational algebra* with its procedures of calculation, its structures, etc; (2) *axiomatic logic*

---

[1] Braine (1962) feels that Piaget has nonetheless succumbed to it.

as the science of truth conditions, or the theory of formalization itself—this we will call pure or formalized logic [p. 23]." Now it happens that the important formalisms coming out of genetic epistemology are axiomatizations. Grize's system for the grouping is an example. Other examples include Grize's later work on the transition between concrete and formal operations (Grize, 1963), the psychology of geometry (Grize, 1964), and the child's notion of time (Grize, 1966). Papert's reformulation of Piaget's theory of formal operations (Papert, 1963) is another example. These axiomatizations may be contrasted with algebraic structures such as Piaget's grouping model of concrete operational thought, whose axiomatic basis was unexplored (not troubled about —Piaget, 1957b, p. 26) until Grize's (1960) paper. The second type of logic Piaget distinguished thus seems to be favored for genetic epistemology. Nonetheless, Piaget expresses a different preference for psychology.

4. FORMALIZATION IN PSYCHOLOGY CHEZ PIAGET

Piaget (1949) considers himself "a psychologist who is interested in logic to the extent that it allows the construction of a pure model of the structures of thought [p. 1]."[2] The formalism should be related to the mental structures roughly the way that mathematical physics is related to experimental physics (Inhelder & Piaget, 1958, p. 271; Piaget, 1952, p. 73; Piaget, 1957b, pp. 25–26). Which of the two types of formalism that Piaget (1957b) distinguished above are suitable for this role? Piaget (1957b) answers that "axiomatic logic is useless for the particular purpose we have in mind. If we wished to formalize psychological *theories* it would be the only suitable method, but our present aim is to disengage the logical structure of psychological or mental *facts* [p. 23]." Instead of axiomatic logic, an algebraic "psycho-logic" must be constructed to study the thought processes (c.f., Piaget, 1952; Mays, 1954). The reason that Piaget, as a psychologist, favors algebraic instead of

[2]As an epistemologist, of course, Piaget has other interests in logic.

axiomatic systems is connected to the fundamental Genevan notion of *operations*. Roughly speaking, operations are mature, reversible, thought processes which must, by their very nature, exist in complex, equilibrated systems, never in isolation (Piaget, 1960; Piaget, 1969b, p. xxvi). Axiomatizations are too rigid and too atomistic to mirror the mobile and holistic character of these operational systems, or *structures d'ensemble* (Piaget, 1952; 1957b, p. 24). Perhaps a more fundamental objection to axiomatization in psychology derives from Piaget's metatheoretical concern with structuralism (Piaget, 1970c). Structures are organized entities with various properties that need not be detailed here. Suffice it to say that Piaget believes human thought forms structures from an early age. As a consequence, only logical systems that are themselves structures can be used to explain mental facts. And Piaget makes it clear that for him axiomatic systems are not structures, for want of certain structural properties (Piaget, 1970c, p. 30).

Not only is axiomatic logic useless for understanding equilibrated thought at a given stage, but it is similarly vain to try to deduce one stage from another, or to deduce the construction of genetically later notions from genetically earlier ones (Piaget, 1942, p. 7). This is because intellectual development proceeds by a *sui generis* process of construction called *reflecting abstraction* (Beth & Piaget, 1961, p. 203) rather than by a process of deduction. As a case in point, the psychological value of Grize's system, whatever that may be, is not tarnished by any attempt on his part to deduce the laws of numbers from groupings. Instead he modifies the axioms for groupings to pass in a psychologically faithful way to axioms for numbers (Grize, 1960, p. 87; c.f., Piaget, 1967a, p. 124).

Instead of axiomatic logic, then, Piaget has built his developmental theories around certain algebraic models that are structures in Piaget's (1970c) technical sense. These models include the three mathematical structures investigated by the French Bourbaki mathematicians (Piaget, 1950a, p. 36f; 1967c, p. 417; 1970b, pp. 24–26), as well as his own invention, the grouping, which Piaget (1942, p. 284) argues is the logical analog of the mathematical group (of the Bourbaki).[3]

Piaget's views of the purely scientific, psychological import of the axiomatization of the grouping are thus quite complex. As part of the program of genetic epistemology—a discipline with roots in psychology—Piaget warmly endorses Grize's work. But in general Piaget evidently holds axiomatization of intellectual structures in disfavor.

The apparent paradox may be resolved with the help of Piaget's discussion of axiomatization in his *Introduction a L'épistemologie génétique* (1950b). Piaget argues there that despite all the liberty mathematicians have in choosing primitive terms, axioms, and rules of inference for their axiomatizations, their completed system is fundamentally tied to psychological operations (c.f. Piaget, 1967b, p. 396). After an argument we will not detail here, Piaget (1950a, T. 1) says:

> The conclusion to which these remarks lead us is therefore that axiomatic construction is more parallel to genetic construction than it seems, although the latter may be freely transformed by axiomatizing it. . . . Indeed, an axiomatization does not bear directly on the operations themselves, but on the propositions which express their results. It is thus the implications between propositions that alone concern the axiomatician, and not the prior [operational] construction. On the contrary, it is these implications between operations themselves which interest the genetician [developmentalist], and this is why the two kinds of investigations are complementary, one bearing on the anterior or implicit connections, doubtless inexhaustable, the other on their formal explication, doubtless always partial [pp. 107–108].

It seems, therefore, that a system such as Grize's is one step removed from the psychological reality of groupings. Each formula of the axiomatization is not itself an operation but expresses the proposition that results from an operation. The deductive relations between formulas seems to reflect, in some way, the psychological relationship between operations. Hence, it may be argued that if our theory can illuminate the in-

---

[3]For Piaget's views on the interpretation of such formalisms into psychological theories, see Piaget and Morf (1958, pp. 51 ff.).

terrelations of the abilities represented by theses of an axiomatization, then it indirectly illuminates the organization of operations in the child's mind. Genevans can only applaud this latter achievement. The question is whether they are bound to believe that Grize's axiomatization, as utilized here, will in fact illuminate mental operations, directly or indirectly. As we have seen, Piaget does believe that axiomatizations are connected to cognition. So it seems he must admit that *if* we have the correct axiom system, and *if* we are using it correctly, then the theory should work. As to our choice of axiom-system, Genevans can have no quarrel with the selection of an axiomatization of the grouping. Piaget (1942, p. 302) refers to groupings as the *sine qua non* of intelligence itself. The groupings are elsewhere said (Piaget, 1957b) to give "an exhaustive catalogue of concrete operations [p. 46]." Moreover, from Piaget's praise of Grize's work, we may infer that Piaget is content with Grize's formalization of the grouping structure. But what objections might be raised to our particular *use* of the axiom system?

5. POSSIBLE GENEVAN OBJECTIONS

Nature of the Tasks

The coordination rule described in Chapter 5 translates the formalism into problems testing class-inclusion and length principles. These latter principles are the concern of two of the most important groupings, I and V (see Flavell, 1963, pp. 173–187 for a summary of the groupings). But perhaps it may be objected that the tasks are not "concrete" enough for concrete operations since they concern abstract logical principles. Problems for concrete operations are generally of a more mundane nature (e.g., the tasks described in Chapter 1, section 1). The complex logical structure of our tasks suggests that they are more germane to the formal operations of adolescence.

But this objection confounds the abstractness of the psychologist's representations of problems given to children with the abstractness of the form of information given to and expected from the child. The concreteness which Inhelder and Piaget (1958, p. 249) see as limiting thought below the level of formal operations concerns the latter issue, not the former. Hence the fact that we decide to write a formula to represent a task given to a child does not bear on the abstractness of the task. Certainly Piaget is himself not reluctant to engage in formalization when discussing children of all developmental levels. As for the tasks themselves, they deal exclusively with objects all of whose relevant properties are known to the child. Even when an attribute is temporarily hidden (the markings underneath the blocks, or the total length of a stick), the familiarization procedure made it clear that the child understood *what* it was that was hidden. As to the verbal nature of the task, Inhelder & Piaget (1958) state that "all verbal thought is not formal and it is possible to get correct reasoning about simple propositions as early as the 7–8 year level, provided that these propositions correspond to sufficiently concrete representations [p. 252]." Our subjects were close to the 7–8 year range, and as just argued our tasks fulfill the concreteness proviso.

Subjects Tested

Perhaps Genevans would make the following objection. Grize's axiomatization is designed to describe groupings, which are a characteristic of concrete operational thought and not characteristic of preoperational thought. Hence we cannot test the model built around Grize's system on preoperational children (since the axiomatization was not built for them) without vitiating any investment Genevan psychology has in the test of the model. That our subjects were at least partially preoperational is shown by the fact that they did not pass all of the tasks based on the grouping system.

But this objection does not follow from the Genevan position. Piaget (1957a; Inhelder & Sinclair, 1969) views the transition from preoperational to concrete operational thought as gradual, with greater and greater equilibrium being attained throughout the preoperational level.[4] It is reasonable to attribute to Piaget the belief that the grouping follows the same gradual course of development as equilibrium since the two concepts are almost interdefinable below the level of formal operations. But if this is the case, the underlying processes reflected by Grize's axioms will mature slowly together, which seems to be the thrust of the notion of structured wholes (cf. Braine, 1959).

Synchrony of Development

But if there is such synchrony in the maturation of the operations, then perhaps Genevans will have a different objection. Since operations mature together, our model is misconceived. It was argued earlier (Ch. 6, section 4) that our model could be tested only by observing the pattern in which tasks became consolidated in the child's repetoire through development. A test of the model thus relies on developmental asynchrony. If the ability to do all the tasks develops at once, albeit slowly, our task-by-task approach is inappropriate. Yet simultaneous development of the abilities seems to be required by the Genevan concept of structured whole.

However, the axiomatic-processes may mature together and yet still be differentially ready to be applied to tasks of different kinds. This possibility would simply be another reflection of the difference between the children's competence and performance, a distinction Genevans take seriously. Pinard and Laurendeau (1969) argue that such *horizontal décalage,* or asynchronism in the development of abilities, even with respect to the same grouping, is not antithetical to the Piagetian position, when the asynchronism occurs before an operational level is fully attained. Inhelder and Sinclair (1969) invoke the same point of view when analyzing the results of their training experiments. Hence our model violates no Genevan postulates in this respect. Anyway, in point of fact our subjects usually passed some but not all of the

[4]This, despite remarks to the contrary in an earlier source about operations being "suddenly grouped" (Piaget, 1950b, pp. 139–140).

tasks; and certain sorts of problems (e.g., those containing subtraction) were more difficult than others. These data show that Grize's axiomatization does not represent a structured whole unless horizontal *decalage* is allowed for.

The Reasoning Process

Another objection that might be raised concerns the plausibility of the child's reasoning from axioms to theorems in the formal, logical way that Grize's axiomatization operates. Surely a child who might still be unsure about the invariance of the mass of a ball of clay through transformation of shape (Piaget & Inhelder, 1941) cannot be expected to deduce logical principles one from the other. Indeed, Grize and Matalon (1962) conclude that even adults do not reason axiomatically, in the sense of starting from tautologies and deducing other tautologies. Rather, they believe, adults start with contingent matters of fact and deduce other facts by means of general rules of inference applying to those facts. Similarly, Piaget (1957b, p. 24) believes that adult thinking cannot be axiomatized, and *a fortiori* neither can the child's. Yet Grize's axiomatization proceeds from logical truth to logical truth, and we might be accused of trying to model in this implausible way the thinking that goes on when one of our children tackles a class-inclusion or length task.

However, our theory nowhere claims that children are deducing theorems from Grize's axioms. Rather, the question asked was only whether the deductive connections within the formalism might parallel the psychological connections between tasks, *whatever* the latter may be. Certainly no suggestion was made that the deductions in the formalism *were* the psychological connections between tasks. The theory, perhaps to its discredit, makes few if any claims about these psycholgical connections.

Having met these objections, can we now conclude that Genevan psychology predicts that a model like ours will be true?

This conclusion still seems unsafe in light of Piaget's serious reservations about axiomatic theories in general. We may only conclude, as said above, that Genevans would predict that if any axiomatic theory such as ours will work, then the most likely candidate is one built around Grize's formalism. After considering some of Piaget's views, how much investment his psychological theories have in the fate of the model described here is a question best left to the individual reader.

But as if the reader's decision were not difficult enough, one last source of complexity must be introduced.

6. CHALLENGE TO GRIZE'S AXIOMATIZATION

Contrary to Piaget's warm endorsement of Grize's axiomatization of the grouping, another logician, G. G. Granger (1965), has decided that Grize's system "raises in its presentation and in its structure, serious difficulties which invalidate it [p. 73]." Granger claims that Grize has failed to capture the grouping Piaget really had in mind as explicated in *Traité de Logique* (1949). When the class-inclusion relation is involved, the grouping should induce a hierarchy of classes similar to a zoological classification. Specifically, Granger demonstrates that Grize has unintentionlly allowed all terms in the system to be composed into another term of the system by means of a binary operation. This circumstance is in plain violation of one principle of Piaget's grouping—as formulated in *Traité de Logique,* at any rate. Piaget (1949) elucidated the principle this way: "But the joining of arbitrary and separate classes does not lead to a class defined by positive characteristics (two 'species' belonging to distinct families do not constitute by themselves a 'class,' etc.) . . . If one joined into a single class the species 'river trout' and 'grey foxes,' the result is not a class belonging to the classification. . . [p. 93]." Granger proceeds to present his own alternative axiomatization, which he claims is free of this defect.

The possibility of using Granger's system as the formal skeleton of our theory, rather than Grize's, is enhanced by the fact that Granger means his axiomatization to have empirical consequences. He writes (1965) that "the proposed formulation appears sufficiently accurate for it to be possible to construct Piagetian experiments allowing us to establish—or to reject— *axiom by axiom* its functional psychological reality [p. 83]." (The emphasis is in the original.) It might seem, then, that we should rely on Granger's formalism instead of Grize's.

But whereas Piaget endorses the work of Grize, and Grize often writes for Piaget's *Etudes d'Epistémologie Génétique,* Granger is not altogether in the Genevan camp. His objections to aspects of the program of genetic epistemology have been criticized by Piaget (1963, pp. 185–191). The issue is further complicated by the fact that Granger's criticisms seem to have had their effect on Grize, who later offered yet another alternative axiomatization of the grouping (Grize, 1967, pp. 519–521). Grize's second version seems to have corrected the problem raised by Granger. It also seems to express better the dichotomous nature of Piaget's groupings (Piaget, 1949).

In the end, we have decided to rely on Grize's original axiomatization. It has received the most attention by Piaget and has been endorsed both before and after Granger's criticism of it. Moreover, our tasks seem to violate Piaget's (1949) restriction on the addition of classes only once (cf. task CA3). The possibility remains that the "wrong" axiomatization, from the Genevan theoretical point of view, has been chosen. If this is the case, then obviously any commitment owed to our model by Piagetians is diluted still further. Whether the right axiomatic system has been chosen form the empirical point of view—and this, of couse, is by far the most important point of view—can be determined only through further experimentation.

12
DIRECTION OF FURTHER THEORETICAL EFFORTS

It would be natural at this point to suggest new axiom-systems to serve as skeletons for further theories of the kind presented in Chapters 6–10. Such theories might bear on additional length abilities possesed by children, should it be the case that Grize's axiomatization does not permit derivation of every principle children comprehend. In addition, the present data suggest that an entirely different set of axioms will be required to explain class-inclusion abilities. Other logical realms, e.g., the properties of subregions of a plane, also seem amenable to the present approach.

However, construction of new theories of this nature will probably be counterproductive, regardless of the accuracy of their predictions. The approach to cognitive development exemplified in this volume seems to the writer unredeemably misconceived. The reason is as follows.

The unsuccessful attempts to construe Chomsky's (1957, 1965) generative grammar as a psychological model of actual sentence production has clarified a general issue concerning psychological theories (Fodor & Garrett, 1966). A model that describes a domain of human abilities need have no direct connection to the internal processes that account for those abilities. The present model attempts to predict the pattern of emergence of certain logical skills in children. Its partial success does not imply that any of its properties will illuminate the real-time mental processes that underlie those abilities. The only feature of the model that could be the analog of those mental processes is the set of formal derivations required for the proof of theorems in Grize's system. Proposing this analogy, however, raises difficult questions about alternative possible proofs, the psychological role of traditional logic in mental derivations, the proper formulation of certain of the axioms in the theory, and so forth. None of this has been worked out.[1] The present model is therefore not a process-model. In one good sense of the term "psychological" it is justifiably denied the description "psychological theory."

For this reason (among others) it seems wise to abandon the present approach to theory construction, in the hope of finding a model closer to the actual mental processes involved in logical inference. In Volume II we turn our backs on the findings and conclusions of Volume I. The crucial competence-performance distinction is reformulated. New data are discussed, and a new theory is proposed.

---

[1]The proposal was even rejected in section 5 of Chapter 11 in return for a defense against a possible Piagetian objection. The point there was that a correspondence between the children's reasoning processes and derivations within the formalism need not be presupposed to account for the accuracy of the model's predictions.

REFERENCES

Beilin, H. The training and acquisition of logical operations. In M.F. Rosskopf, L.P. Steffe, & S. Taback (Eds.), *Piagetian cognitive-development research and mathematical education*. Washington, D.C.: National Council of Teachers of Mathematics, 1971.

Beth, E.W., A propos d'un "Traite de Logique." *Methodos*, 1950, **2** (6-7), 258-264.

Beth, E.W., & Piaget, J. *Études d'épistémologie génétique*. Vol. 14. *Épistémologie mathématique et psychologie*. Paris: Presses Universitaires de France, 1961.

Braine, M.D.S. The ontogeny of certain logical operations: Piaget's formulation examined by non-verbal methods. *Psychological Monographs*, 1959, **73** (5, Whole No. 475).

Braine, M.D.S. Piaget on reasoning: A methodological critique and alternative proposals. In W. Kessen & C. Kuhlman (Eds.), *Thought in the young child*. Chicago: University of Chicago Press, 1962.

Braine, M.D.S. Development of a grasp of transitivity of length: A reply to Smedslund. *Child Development*, 1964, **35**, 799-810.

Bruner, J.S., Goodnow, J.J. & Austin, G.A. *A study of thinking*. New York: Wiley, 1956.

Bruner, J.S., Olver, R.R., & Greenfield, P.M., et al. *Studies in cognitive growth*. New York: Wiley, 1966.

Bryant, P.E., & Trabasso, T. Can "preoperational" children make transitive inferences? Unpublished manuscript, Princeton University, 1970.

Chomsky, N. *Syntactic structures*. The Hague: Mouton, 1957.

Chomsky, N. *Aspects of the theory of syntax*. Cambridge, Mass.: MIT Press, 1965.

Chomsky, N. *Language and mind*. New York: Harcourt, Brace & World, 1968.

Copi, I.M. *Symbolic logic*. New York: Macmillan, 1967.

Elkind, D. Discrimination, seriation, and numeration of size and dimensional differences in young children: Piaget replication study VI. *The Journal of Genetic Psychology*, 1964, **104**, 275-296.

Flavell, J.H. *The developmental psychology of Jean Piaget*. Princeton, N.J.: Van Nostrand, 1963.

Flavell, J.H., & Wohlwill, J.F. Formal and functional aspects of cognitive development. In D. Elkind & J.H. Flavell (Eds.), *Studies in cognitive development: Essays in honor of Jean Piaget*. New York: Oxford University Press, 1969.

Fodor, J.A., & Garrett, M. Some reflections on competence and performance. In J. Lyons & R.J. Wales (Eds.), *Psycholinguistics papers*. Edinburgh: Edinburgh University Press, 1966.

Furth, H.G. *Piaget and knowledge*. Englewood Cliffs, N.J.: Prentice Hall, 1969.

Granger, G. Un probléme d'axiomatisation en psychologie. *Logique et Analyse*, 1965, **8,** 72-83.

Grize, J.B. Du groupement au nombre: Essai de formalisation. In P. Greco, J. Grize, S. Papert, & J. Piaget, *Études d'épistémologie génétique*. Vol. 11. *Problemes de la construction du nombre*. Paris: Presses Universitaires de France, 1960.

Grize, J.B. Des groupments a l'algebre de Boole: Essai de filiation des structures logiques. In L. Apostel, J.B. Grize, S. Papert, & J. Piaget, *Études d'épistémologie génétique*. Vo. 15. *La filiation des structures*. Paris: Presses Universitaires de France, 1963.

Grize, J.B. Essai d'une formalisation du temps non-metrique à partir des données psychogénétiques. In J.B. Grize, K. Henry, M. Meylan-Backs, F. Orsini, J. Piaget, & N. Van den Bogaert-Rombouts, *Études d'épistémologie génétique*. Vol. 20. *L'épistémologie du temps*. Paris: Presses Universitaires de France, 1966, 107-136.

Grize, J.B. Remarque sur l'epistemologie mathématique des nombres naturels. In *Logique et connaissance scientifique: Encyclopedia de la Pleiade*. Paris: Gallimard, 1967.

Grize, J.B., & Matalon, B. Introduction a une étude experimentale et formelle du raisonnement naturel. In E.W. Beth, J.B. Grize, R. Martin, B. Matalon, A. Naess, & J. Piaget, *Études d'épistémologie génétique*. Vol. 16. *Implication formalisation, et logique naturelle*. Paris: Presses Universitaires de France, 1962.

Hempel, C.G. Review of Jean Piaget, *Logic and Psychology*. *The Journal of Symbolic Logic*, 1960, **25,** (3) 256-257.

Inhelder, B., & Piaget, J. *The growth of logical thinking from childhood to adolescence*. New York: Basic Books, 1958.

Inhelder, B., & Piaget, J. *The early growth of logic in the child*. New York: W.W. Norton, 1964.

Inhelder, B., & Sinclair, H. Learning cognitive structures. In P.H. Mussen, J. Langer, & M. Covington (Eds.), *Trends and issues in developmental psychology*. New York: Holt, Rinehart & Winston, 1969.

Kneale, W., Review of Jean Piaget, *Traité de Logique*. *The Philosophical Quarterly*, 1952, **2** (6), 91-93.

Kohnstamm, G.A. An evaulation of part of Piaget's theory. *Acta Psychologica,* 1963, **21,** 313-315.

Kohnstamm, G.A. *Piaget's analysis of class inclusion: Right or wrong?* The Hague: Mouton, 1967.

Kofsky, E. A scalogram study of classification development. *Child Development,* 1966, **37,** 191-204.

Mays, W. The epistemology of Professor Piaget. *Proceedings of the Aristotelian Society,* 1954, **54,** 49-76.

McKinsey, J. Reviews of assorted logic papers by Piaget. *The Journal of Symbolic Logic,* 1943, **8** (2), 57-58.

Morf, A. Apprentissage d'une structure logique concrète (inclusion): Effets et limites. In A. Morf, J. Smedslund, Vinh-Bang, & J.F. Wohlwill, *Études d'épistémologie génétique.* Vol. 9. *L'apprentissage des structures logique.* Paris: Presses Universitaires de France, 1959,

Murray J.P., & Youniss, J. Achievement of inferential transitivity and its relation to serial ordering. *Child Development,* 1968, **39,** 1259-1268.

Papert, S. Şur la logique Piagetienne. In L. Apostel, J. Grize, S. Papert, & J. Piaget, *Études d'épistemologie génétique.* Vol 15. *La filiation des structures.* Paris: Presses Universitaires de France, 1963.

Parsons, C. Inhelder and Piaget's *The Growth of Logical Thinking:* A logician's viewpoint. *British Journal of Psychology,* 1960, **51** (1), 75–84.

Piaget, J. *Classes, relations et nombres: Essai sur les groupements de la logistique et sur la reversibilitie de la pensee.* Paris: Vrin, 1942.

Piaget, J. *Traité de logique.* Paris: Colin, 1949.

Piaget, J. *Introduction a l'épistémologie génétique.* Vol. 1. Paris: Presses Universitaires de France, 1950.(a)

Piaget, J. *The psychology of intelligence.* London: Routledge, 1950.(b)

Piaget, J. La logistique axiomatique ou "pure," la logistique opératoire ou psychologique et les realité auxquelles elles correspondent. *Methodos* (Milan), 1952, **4,** 72–84.

Piaget, J. Logique et équilibre dans les comportements du sujet. In L. Apostel, B. Mandelbrot, & J Piaget, *Études d'épistemologie génétique.* Vol. 12. *Logique et equilibre.* Paris: Presses Universitaires de France, 1957. (a)

Piaget, J. *Logic and psychology.* New York: Basic Books, 1957. (b)

Piaget, J. Programme et methods de l'épistemologie génétique. In W. E. Beth, W. Mays, & J. Piaget, *Études d'épistemologie génétique.* Vol. 1. *Épistémologie genetique et recherche psychologique.* Paris: Presses Universitaires de France, 1957. (c)

Piaget, J. Defense de l'épistémologie génétique. In E. Beth, J. Grize, R. Martin, B. Matalon, A. Naess, & J. Piaget, *Études d'éspistémologie génétique*. Vol. 15. *La filiation des structures*. Paris: Presses Universitaires de France, 1963.

Piaget, J. *The child's conception of number*. New York: W. W. Norton, 1965.

Piaget, J. Methodes de l'épistémologie. In *Logique et connaissance scientifique: Encyclopedie de la Pléiade*. Paris: Gallimard, 1967. (a)

Piaget, J. Epistemologie de la logique. In *Logique et connaissance scientifique: Encyclopedie de la Pleiade*. Paris: Gallimard, 1967. (b)

Piaget, J. Mathematiques: Les donnés génétiques. In *Logique et connaissance scientifique: Encyclopedie de la Pleiade*. Paris: Gallimard, 1967. (c)

Piaget, J. *Six psychological studies*. New York: Vintage Books, 1967. (d)

Piaget, J. *The mechanisms of perception*. New York: Basic Books, 1969. (a)

Piaget, J. *The child's conception of time*. New York: Basic Books, 1969. (b)

Piaget, J. *Psychologie et épistémologie*. Paris: Denoel, 1970. (a)

Piaget, J. *Genetic epistemology*. New York: Columbia University Press, 1970. (b)

Piaget, J. *Structuralism*. New York: Basic Books, 1970. (c)

Piaget, J., & Inhelder, B. *Le développement des quantités chez l'enfant*. Neuchâtel: Delachaux et Niestle, 1941.

Piaget, J., & Inhelder, B. *The child's conception of space*. New York: W. W. Norton, 1967.

Piaget, J., & Inhelder, B. *The psychology of the child*. New York: Basic Books, 1969.

Piaget, J., Inhelder, B., & Szeminska, A. *The child's conception of geometry*. New York: Basic Books, 1960.

Piaget, J., & Morf, A. Les isomorphismes partiels entre les structures logiques et les structures perceptives. In J. Bruner, F. Bresson, A. Morf, & J. Piaget, *Études d'épistémologie génétique*. Vol. 6. *Logique et perception*. Paris: Presses Universitaires de France, 1958. Pp. 49–116.

Pinard, A., & Laurendeau, M. "Stage" in Piaget's cognitive-developmental theory: Exegesis of a concept. In D. Elkind & J. H. Flavell (Eds.), *Studies in cognitive development: Essays in honor of Jean Piaget*. New York: Oxford University Press, 1969.

Quine, W. V. O. Reviews of assorted logic papers by Piaget. *The Journal of Symbolic Logic*, 1940, **5** (4), 157.

Siegel, L. S. Development of the concept of seriation. *Developmental Psychology*, 1972, **6** (1), 135-137.

Smedslund, J. The acquisition of conservation of substance and weight in children: I. Introduction. *Scandinavian Journal of Psychology*, 1961, **2,** 11–20.

Smedslund, J. Development of concrete transitivity of length in children. *Child Development*, 1963, **34,** 389–405.

Smedslund, J. Development of a grasp of transitivity of length: A comment on Braine's reply. *Child Development*, 1965, **36,** 577–580.

Smedslund, J. Performance on measurement and pseudomeasurement tasks by five- to seven-year-old children. *Scandinavian Journal of Psychology*, 1966, **7**(2), 81–92.

Stoll, R. R. *Set theory and logic.* San Francisco: W. H. Freeman, 1963.

Suppes, P. *Introduction to logic.* Princeton, N.J.: Van Nostrand, 1957.

Tolman, E. C. *Purposive behavior in animals and men.* New York: Appleton-Century-Crofts, 1932.

Vygotsky, L. *Thought and language.* Cambridge, Mass.: MIT Press, 1962.

Wales, R. J., & Grieve, R. What is so difficult about negation? *Perception & Psychophysics,* 1969, **6,** 327–331.

Wason, P. C. The processing of positive and negative information. *Quarterly Journal of Experimental Psychology,* 1959, **11,** 92–107.

Wason, P. C. Response to affirmative and negative binary statements. *British Journal of Psychology,* 1961, **52**(a), 133–142.

APPENDIXES

APPENDIX I
Proofs of Theorems

LEMMA: Replacement rule for $+$:

$$(x = y) \rightarrow (\ldots x \ldots) = (\ldots y \ldots)$$

Proof: By induction requiring A1, A2, A3, and A17.

T1: $(\,(x = y) \,\&\, (y = z)\,) \rightarrow (x = z)$

Proof: A1, A11

T2: $(x = y) \rightarrow (\,(x + z) = (y + z)\,)$

Proof: A3, A11

T3: $(x + x) = x$

Proof: 1. $x \leqslant x$ A8
        2. $(x + x) = x$ 1, A4

T4: $(x \leqslant z \,\&\, y \leqslant z) \rightarrow x + y \leqslant z$

Proof: 1. $x \leqslant z$ Hypothesis
        2. $y \leqslant z$ Hypothesis
        3. $(x + z) = z$ 1, A4
        4. $(y + z) = z$ 2, A4
        5. $x + (y + z) = z$ 3, 4,
                                  Lemma
        6. $(x + y) + z = z$ 5, A9
        7. $(x + y) \leqslant z$ 6, A7

T5: $x \leqslant y \rightarrow (x - z \leqslant y - z)$

Proof: 1. $x \leqslant y$ Hypothesis
2. $y \leqslant (z + (y - z))$ A6
3. $x \leqslant (z + (y - z))$ 1, 2, A1
4. $(x - z) \leqslant (y - z)$ 3, A5

T6: $x \leqslant y \rightarrow (z - y \leqslant z - x)$

Proof: 1. $x \leqslant y$ Hypothesis
2. $x + (z - x) \leqslant y + (z - x)$
          1, A3
3. $z \leqslant (x + (z - x))$ A6
4. $z \leqslant (y + (z - x))$ 2, 3, A1
5. $(z - y) \leqslant (z - x)$ 4, A5

T7: $(x \leqslant w) \& ((w + y) \leqslant z) \rightarrow (x + y) \leqslant z$

Proof: 1. $x \leqslant w$ Hypothesis
2. $(w + y) \leqslant z$ Hypothesis
3. $(x + y) \leqslant (w + y)$ 1, A3
4. $(x + y) \leqslant z$ 2, 3, A1

T8: $(x = y) \rightarrow (x - y = 0)$

Proof:[1] 1. $x = y$ Hypothesis
2. $x \leqslant y$ 1, A11
3. $(x + 0) \leqslant (y + 0)$ 2, A3
4. $0 \leqslant x$ A10
5. $(0 + x) = x$ 4, A4
6. $(x + 0) = x$ 5, A2
7. $x \leqslant (y + 0)$ 6, 3 Lemma
8. $(x - y) \leqslant 0$ 7, A5
9. $0 \leqslant x - y$ A10
11. $0 = x - y$ 8, 9, A11

---

[1] D. Paul Snyder suggested this proof.

APPENDIX II

The following remarks will be helpful to the reader not familiar with the conventions for grouping and punctuation within formulas.

Variables like x and y represent objects of an abstract sort, e.g., classes or lengths. An expression like "$x + y$" or "$x - y$" stands for an operation on these objects. For example, under one interpretation of the symbols "x," "y," and "$+$," the expression "$x + y$" might symbolize the union of two classes. It is important to realize that the union of two classes, a and b, is itself a class, namely, the class $a \cup b$. A class is different than a statement. A statement can be true or false; a class can never be true or false. So $a \cup b$ is not a statement, but an object. Similarly, "$x + y$" and "$x - y$" are not statements.

The symbols "$\leqslant$," "$\leqslant_1$," and "$=$" represent relations that hold between objects. The expression "$x \leqslant y$" says that the relation $\leqslant$ holds between the things x and y. If x and y are classes, for example, and "$\leqslant$" represents inclusion, then the expression "$x \leqslant y$" would mean that the class x is included in the class y. Thus "$x \leqslant y$"—unlike "x," "$x + y$," etc.—is a statement, capable of being either true or false.

The symbols "$\&$," "v," "$\rightarrow$," and "$\leftrightarrow$" connect statements only. They do not connect objects. Thus, the expression "$x \& y$" makes no sense in our notation. Similarly, the symbol "$-$" for negation applies only to statements. To illustrate, the formula "$x \leqslant y \& w \leqslant z$" says that the two statements "$x \leqslant y$" and "$w \leqslant z$" are true.

These considerations indicate how formulas in Grize's system should be read, and enable us to omit extra sets of parentheses. The following are examples of formulas in the text, along with the same formulas written with additional parentheses.

a. $(x \leqslant y \,\&\, y \leqslant z) \rightarrow (x \leqslant z)$
b. $((x \leqslant y) \,\&\, (y \leqslant z)) \rightarrow (x \leqslant z)$

a. $(x \leqslant y) \rightarrow (x + z \leqslant y + z)$
b. $(x \leqslant y) \rightarrow ((x + z) \leqslant (y + z))$

a. $x + y = y + x$
b. $(x + y) = (y + x)$

a. $(w \leqslant x \,\&\, x + y \leqslant z) \rightarrow (w + y \leqslant z)$
b. $((w \leqslant x) \,\&\, ((x + y) \leqslant z)) \rightarrow ((w + y) \leqslant z)$

a. $(x + y \leqslant z) \rightarrow (x + y \leqslant z - y)$
b. $((x + y) \leqslant z) \rightarrow ((x + y) \leqslant (z - y))$

INDEXES

AUTHOR INDEX

Numbers in *italics* refer to the pages on which the complete references are listed.

SUBJECT INDEX

DATE DUE